Community and the Northwestern Logger

Rural Studies Series

Community and the Northwestern Logger

Continuities and Changes in the Era of the Spotted Owl

Matthew S. Carroll

Foreword by Don A. Dillman

Westview Press

BOULDER • SAN FRANCISCO • OXFORD

Rural Studies Series, Sponsored by the Rural Sociological Society

Published in 1995 in the United States of America by Westview Press, Inc., 5500 Central Avenue, Boulder, Colorado 80301-2877, and in the United Kingdom by Westview Press, 12 Hid's Copse Road, Cumnor Hill, Oxford OX2 9JJ

Library of Congress Cataloging-in-Publication Data
Carroll, Matthew S. (Matthew Stephen)
    Community and the Northwestern logger : continuities and changes in the era of the spotted owl / by Matthew S. Carroll ; foreword by Don A. Dillman
        p.   cm. — (Rural Studies Series of the Rural Sociological Society)
    Includes bibliographical references and index.
    ISBN 0-8133-8818-X
    1. Loggers—Northwest, Pacific—Social conditions.   2. Forest management—Economic aspects—Northwest, Pacific.   3. Forest management—Environmental aspects—Northwest, Pacific.
    4. Northwest, Pacific—Rural conditions.   I. Title.   II. Series.
    HD8039.L92U533   1995
    338.1'7498'09795—dc20   94-42047
                                                                                                                      CIP

Printed and bound in the United States of America

∞   The paper used in this publication meets the requirements of the American National Standard for Permanence of Paper for Printed Library Materials Z39.48-1984.

10   9   8   7   6   5   4   3   2   1

This book is dedicated to the three most influential people in my life:

--To my father Jim Carroll (1925-1986), consummate outdoorsman, pragmatic philosopher, and natural leader, who taught me to love the outdoors and to admire and respect working people and their store of knowledge and wisdom;

--To my mother, Marge Carroll, font of warmth, stability, and love of life to all who know her, who taught me about understanding people at an intuitive level and to love music and dancing;

--To my spouse and lifemate, Denise Konetchy, animal lover, horsewoman, veterinarian, and organizer of people, who has taught me more about the important things--constancy, commitment and balance --than a lifetime of academic training could ever provide. It is she who constantly reminds me by words, and especially by example, that there is life beyond work and the academy.

CONTENTS

FOREWORD

Virtually everyone in the United States has heard of the spotted owl. Its image has appeared frequently on the covers of national magazines, and its habits have been the object of multiple expensive scientific investigations. Simultaneously, this tiny creature is seen as mysterious, pretty, delicate, dignified, and threatened with extinction.

Less visible to and less understood by Americans are the lives of those who have frequently been portrayed as the spotted owl's enemy-- the northwestern loggers.

This book is not about right and wrong, nor which values should prevail in this divisive controversy; neither is it about how the forest industry works. Rather, it is about the social world of loggers and how that world has been affected by the dispute. The book also provides important background for the development of policies essential for finding reasonable and humane accommodations in forestry and natural resource conflicts, of which the spotted owl dilemma happens to be the one with greatest visibility.

The reader is introduced to the lives of working loggers from their perspectives as gyppos, fallers, choker setters, landing chasers, yarders, cat skinners, and other jobs associated with transforming trees into lumber. The author's experiences of working on a logging crew produce engaging descriptions of logging work: for example, how a "talkie tooter" enables a rigging slinger to control the operation of a yarder. Intriguing as these descriptions of the logger's world are, they are only prologue to the author's purpose.

Community, as a sociological concept, has been used to describe influences on people's lives that go beyond family, clubs, organizational connections, friendship groups, and work. It influences how people think of themselves and define life possibilities. Traditionally, community has been defined by a named geographic place. Development of the mass society in this century meant that geographic community became less important in most people's lives and produced sociological debate over whether anything has taken the place of the geographically bounded community as an anchor in people's lives.

Here, the author shows that indeed loggers are part of a community around which they build strong identities and equally powerful, even fierce, loyalties. However, this occupational community is not geographically centered around a specific town. Rather it exists over a somewhat broader area across which particular loggers typically work. The analysis suggests that the logger's occupational community provides the basis of reference group, pride in work, friendship support in hard times, and ultimately the sense of self.

When hundreds of thousands of farmers were being forced out of agriculture in the early 1980s, the plight of many was made especially difficult because for generations their families had farmed, and it had become a way of life. For them to even conceive of being retrained for other kinds of work was a wrenching experience. Many could not imagine being anything other than a farmer. Recognizing this social fact was an essential prerequisite to successful job training efforts.

Matt Carroll, in this book, contributes to our understanding of the lives of loggers what Bill and Judy Heffernan and other rural sociologists did for farmers and the difficult agricultural transition more than a decade ago. He provides a sociological understanding of their work and community, both of which are essential prerequisites for intelligent adjustment policies. Along the way he contributes to our understanding of how "community" influences human behavior. He also brings to the community literature an important study from a region of the United States which appears only infrequently in the rural sociological literature.

And, finally, he intertwines the rich tradition of past research, new research data, and policy considerations in a way that is much talked about but seldom achieved in practice.

Don A. Dillman
Washington State University

ACKNOWLEDGMENTS

The material in this volume reflects two separate research projects and associated writing which took place over a more than twelve year period. As one might expect for such an extended project, there are many people who contributed along the way and who are deserving of acknowledgment and thanks. Although he would interpret the policy implications of these studies in a somewhat different light than has been done here, Bob Lee was instrumental in both studies presented in this volume. Bob provided the original inspiration and much advice concerning the conceptualization and conduct of the initial study (i.e., material presented mostly in Chapters 4, 5, and 6). Among other contributions, he served as lead principal investigator for the later social impact study from which the results specifically relating to loggers and their families are drawn and presented in Chapter 7. Another scholar with a major impact on the studies conducted for this monograph is Kristin (Kaela) Warren. Kaela and I functioned as a team in conducting the fieldwork for the impact study, and her insights have been extremely valuable. (For a more complete discussion of the impact study, see Lee, Carroll, and Warren, 1991.)

Ed Gross also played a key role at the conceptual stage of the research and helped to interpret the results of the earlier study, while MaryLou Chopelas and Scott Comstock provided much help and support during the fieldwork. The data collection for the earlier study was partially funded by Resources for the Future. The Northwest Policy Center at the University of Washington provided funding for the impact study, and the Agricultural Research Center and the Department of Natural Resource Sciences at Washington State University supported further analysis and writing time. Don Dillman, Keith Blatner, and my department chair, Ed Depuit, provided crucial support and advice in the later stages of manuscript development. Steve Daniels, my principal academic collaborator, contributed significantly to my thinking, particularly relative to issues discussed in

Chapters 3 and 8 and the Epilogue. Andrea Brandenburg taught me much about the concepts of place and place attachment. Rick Krannich and the late (and sorely missed) Ken Wilkinson provided very helpful reviews of earlier drafts of the manuscript. Andy Deseran of the Rural Studies Series and Kellie Masterson and Julia Joun of Westview have been very helpful and affirming in guiding me through the publication process; Claudia Peck has been superb as a copy editor; and Sharon Gosselin provided invaluable assistance in formatting. Of course, the interpretations presented (and particularly any errors) are ultimately my responsibility.

A group that deserves to be singled out for special thanks are the loggers and their families and other local residents in the field sites who gave so unselfishly of their time and insights during both studies. It would be difficult to find a more generous or good-hearted group of people than the loggers and other residents of forested places of the Pacific Northwest.

A portion of the material in Chapters 4, 5, and 6 appeared previously (in greatly abbreviated form) in an article entitled *Taming the Lumberjack Revisited* published in Volume Two (1988) of *Society and Natural Resources* and in Chapter 11 of Lee, Field, and Burch (1990) which is entitled *Occupational Community and Identity Among Pacific Northwestern Loggers: Implications for Adapting to Economic Changes*. I am grateful to the respective publishers, and in the second case my co-author, for permission to use the material here.

Matthew S. Carroll

1

Community and the Northwestern Logger

Thank you. Mr. President, Vice President Gore, members of the Cabinet, fellow participants in the Forest Conference.

My ministry as Archbishop of Seattle brings me to nearly 200 parishes and Catholic communities from the Canadian border to the Columbia River, and the crest of the Cascade Mountains to the shores of the Pacific. I often drive down Highway 101 from our Parish of St. Anne's from the Olympic Peninsula town of Forks to our Lady of Good Health, our parish in the Grey's Harbor town of Hoquiam. En route I pass through the magnificent moss-covered old-growth forest of the Olympic National Park, pristine forest, virtually untouched by human hands.

I also pass through private and public lands that have been logged and logged again. Some of these lands have been replanted and the uniform group of Douglas firs awaits some future harvest. Other lands are clear-cut and fallow, all but devoid of the abundant forest life which God has graced creation.

At the end of my drive I arrived in Hoquiam, a proud and independent town that carries on despite the recent closure of the mill that was its biggest employer. Here I meet a burly, strapping fellow in the prime of life. He has worked most of the 40 some years in the woods felling trees. He has been without work for months, stretching into years. He has lost his home, and his ties to family and friends. "Archbishop," he asks me, "do you know what it's like to work for 20 years and then end up sleeping in your pickup at the side of the road?" I tell him honestly, "I do not."

But I do know that this man's tragedy has been repeated thousands of times by workers who have lost their livelihoods in our forests. These are not only personal experiences; they are community tragedies. The man who lives in his pickup truck has lost the wherewithal and the self-worth that builds community. He does not vote. He does not belong to the Rotary Club or Kiwanis. He doesn't show up for coffee at the diner or McDonald's.

The loss of that man and those like him is evident in the empty storefronts in downtown Hoquiam and other timber communities. The loss is evident in the lines at the soup kitchens and the welfare office, and the loss is evidence in the homes where unemployed workers, anxious, depressed, sunken despair, lash out at their loved ones or find solace in alcohol or drugs.

A culture, a way of life, prized and reverenced in our timber communities, is dying. I speak today as a representative of the Judeo-Christian tradition that values all of God's creation: the forest, the workers, the workers who labor in the forest, and the communities whose livelihood has been dependent on the forests. In the creation account, the Bible tells us, "God looked at everything that was made and found it very good," and it is.

Mr. President, I commend you for convening this conference. I believe that only through dialogue and full participation of all concerned parties can we achieve a balanced solution that serves the common good. The role of the church is to raise the moral values involved in preserving forests, employing forest workers and saving forest-dependent communities. Our hope is that common ground will be discovered so that the common good will be achieved. The timber crisis is a moral issue. I, the members of my church and the members of many other churches, stand ready to assist your efforts toward resolution and reconciliation. Thank you for listening today. May the blessings of a good and gracious God be with all of us and grant us the wisdom to find solutions.

The Most Reverend Thomas Murphey,
Archbishop of Seattle

Archbishop Murphey's words, spoken at the beginning of President Clinton's forest conference held in Portland, Oregon on April 2, 1993, capture a human side of a long-standing, bitter dispute over the old-growth forests of the Pacific Northwest. The dispute, which has captured the attention of a worldwide audience, has involved the interests and values of many groups. It is fair to say, however, that no group has felt a more direct impact of the issue than the workers and the families of workers who have made their living harvesting those forests. This book is about those workers and their way of life in a rapidly changing world.

The occupation of logging, particularly that in the Pacific Northwest, has long been a subject of interest for many observers of American society. Along with cowboys, hard rock miners and oil wildcatters, loggers are the embodiment of the rugged individualist ethic that is so much a part of the heritage of European settlement of the North American continent. Yet the world has changed around the people who make their living by the extraction or harvest of natural resources. Such workers have become a minority, almost an oddity in a working world made up of a larger and larger group of information processors and service employees. It is not uncommon to read articles about loggers and their families in the press, and in popular literature, written as human interest stories for an urban audience. The very fact that loggers are a subject of such stories because their lives are so different from those led by most Americans, suggests that much has been altered in society since the time when the majority of the American workforce was engaged in extraction or agriculture.

As we noted above, in addition to feeling the effects of long-term social and economic change, loggers in the Pacific Northwest have recently found themselves at the center of an intense national controversy over the future of the region's old-growth Douglas-fir forests. The issue came to a head over the habitat requirements of the northern spotted owl. The owl, an inhabitant of the Douglas-fir old-growth forests was added to the federal government's list of "threatened" species in 1992, under the provisions of the federal Endangered Species Act. This action served to accelerate an already heated dispute over the future of such forests, a dispute that captured public interest as scenes of Douglas-fir forests and loggers at work became commonplace on the evening news. Political attention to the issue and subsequent media attention, created a polarization much like the abortion debate. As this is written, the effects of the controversy, and its aftermath, on the way of life in Northwestern logging communities remains an item of wide public interest.

A question that goes beyond this particular controversy, however, and one that does not lend itself to dramatic portrayal in thirty second sound bites, is what is becoming of the Northwestern logger in the advanced industrial society? Whither the logger in the age of a global economy, increased population pressure on the land base, and unprecedented concern and activism over the environment? How is the fate of these workers and their families and communities linked to broad political social and economic trends? How are the circumstances faced by this group comparable to those of other workers caught in the midst of dramatic change? These were the broad questions of interest when the research to be described here was first conceived.

The inquiry began several years before the spotted owl controversy, with questions centered on how changes in forest land management and regulation of harvest were affecting the modern day logger. Forest policy makers have long been concerned with the effects of forest management on the "stability" of forest dependent human communities, particularly in the Pacific Northwest. The idea of this research was to examine one segment of such communities, the woods workers themselves. As events transpired, the specific focus of the work turned to the impact of the emerging spotted owl/old-growth forest controversy in the region.

Recent Economic and Social/Political Changes

The circumstances faced by modern loggers and many other rural workers as well, are best understood in the context of economic and social/political trends that have been affecting western society for decades. Before proceeding with a discussion of the current studies, it will be useful to step back and briefly examine some of the larger societal forces influencing the changes they face. Building on the work of Drucker (1986), the current author and a colleague have suggested elsewhere (Carroll and Daniels, 1993) that three interrelated developments in the world economy are profoundly influencing the primary producers of natural resource commodities.

The first of these is that the primary products economy has become "uncoupled" from the industrial economy. Drucker cites as an example the changes in the role of agriculture in the U.S. economy. When the national agricultural policy was developed during the Progressive and New Deal eras, farmers constituted nearly one-third of the population and their income amounted to about twenty-five percent of the gross national product (GNP). Their purchases of equipment were a major force in the manufacturing economy. Currently, farmers constitute less than five percent of the population and their income constitutes less than five percent of the GNP. Thus, the linkage between agriculture (arguably the most significant portion of the primary production economy) and the overall economic health of the nation is weaker and less perceptible, despite the obvious critical importance of food to society.

The second development identified is the "uncoupling" of production in the industrial economy from employment. Drucker points out that industrialized countries have, in the last three decades, increased production while decreasing employment. Technical knowledge in the form of automated and less labor intensive technologies have been substituted for labor nearly across the board in the manufacturing sector.

The third development is the increased complexity of economic linkages:

> Finally, the world economy has become harder to understand as it has grown more intricate and internationalized. There are more processing, financing, transporting, marketing, and waste disposal links in the modern industrialized economy. . . Primary production is just one link among many equals, each one being necessary to efficient economic function. Moreover, a complete understanding of one's role as an economic agent requires an international perspective. Capital and information are flowing instantaneously around the globe, and producers must transcend national boundaries as they consider potential markets and competitors (Carroll and Daniels, 1993: 14).

The paper goes on to suggest that the interpretation of these developments can be attributed to the fact that employment in the forest products industry is declining in significance relative to the overall economy, and that, in the long-term, political support is decreasing for programs that promote employment in primary production. Returning to Drucker:

> Another implication of the "uncoupling" of manufacturing production for manufacturing employment is. . . that the choice between an industrial policy that favors industrial *production* and one that favors industrial employment is going to be a singularly contentious political issue for the rest of this century (Drucker, 1986: 780).

As we will discuss throughout this volume, the problems faced by Northwestern loggers and their communities relative to these trends are substantial, even for those not directly affected by the owl issue. Forest products workers have been caught in an economic dilemma that has been particularly visible since the early 1980's due in large part to the economic "uncouplings" noted above. As Hibbard (1992) states:

> Pacific Northwest mill towns and their residents are trapped. Across the region, many outmoded, labor intensive small town mills are being closed. In part this is a response to the timber supply crisis of the early 1990s. But the longer term cause is that older mills are being replaced by a smaller number of modern, more capital intensive mills. In aggregate, the region has the capacity to produce the same product in 1990 as it did in 1980, but with only three-quarters as many mills and two-thirds as many workers.
> From a larger perspective that may be a good thing; The overall efficiency and competitive position of the region's timber industry has been improved. However, mill towns and their residents face a different

calculus. The source of their livelihood, the mills, is disappearing (Hibbard, 1992: 12).[1]

It should be noted, however, that the circumstances faced by Northwestern loggers relative to automation and technology are somewhat different than that faced by millworkers. As we will discuss below, the region's loggers were certainly affected in a dramatic way by a prolonged depression in the industry in the early 1980s. However, although there has apparently been little published economic analysis specifically on the subject, it does not appear that improved technology has, by itself, eliminated jobs in the woods to the degree it has in the mills (Stier, 1982). Labor savings accruing from advances in technology might, in fact, be largely offset in the future by by the need to harvest smaller logs in steeper, less accessible locations, to execute the more complicated harvest patterns required by more environmentally sensitive forest management prescriptions, and to take greater care to leave the harvest sites in better condition (Daniels, 1992a).

One economic pattern that clearly affects both Northwestern loggers *and* millworkers is the movement of wood production capital out of the region (largely to the Southeastern U.S.), a trend that has been in evidence for at least two decades (Young and Newton, 1980; Hibbard, 1992; Hibbard and Elias, 1993). The reasons for "capital flight" are complex and related to a number of influences, including the global economic trends noted above; the availability, age classes, and volumes of public and private timber supplies; and complex interactions between corporate and public policy decision-making. These issues and their impacts on forest workers will be revisited in later chapters.

One social/political trend that has had an obvious and profound effect on forest workers is the rise of environmentalism in the larger society. Much has been written on this subject from both a philosophical and political standpoint (Oelschaeger, 1991; Hays, 1987). Recently Buttel (1992) has provided an analysis that focuses specifically on the rise of environmental politics and its relationship to rural social change. Buttel's analysis seems particularly useful in helping to understand the circumstances faced by Northewestern forest workers.

Buttel goes beyond previous analysis describing the rise of environmentalism as simply a product of society's increased understanding and concern about environmental problems (Milbrath, 1985). He argues that the rise of environmentalism as a *political* force is largely product of fundamental changes in the political coalitions that have governed many western nations in recent decades. He contends that the rise of environmental politics came about in the context of relative economic stagnation in western economies after the post World

War II boom. The hallmark of this period (as Drucker also argued) was increased automation. This, according to Buttel, led to a decline of the power of labor unions and ultimately to a shrinkage of the working class. These events marked the end of the era in which labor was a countervailing force to the political and economic power of industry.

Buttel's analysis goes on to suggest that the sources of political mobilization in society left behind by labor unions and their political representatives are being taken by "new social movements" (NSMs). These NSMs consist mainly of professionals, service workers, and other younger, typically well educated people, generally urban and outside the corporate world. Examples of NSMs include the peace movement, the womens' movement and notably, the environmental movement. What is critically different about the NSMs according to this argument is not just the issues they choose, but that they represent a very different mode of organization than was the case in the working class parties of the earlier era.

Buttel goes on to suggest that the environmental movement is evolving to become "the political center of gravity" of new social movements with the environment as "the master NSM" issue. He notes three significant tendencies in political decision-making related to these changes. The first of these is the "packaging" of environmental reforms within comprehensive frameworks, rather than the more piecemeal approach typical in populist political proposals. The second is to rely heavily on "instrumental-scientific rationality . . . by transforming scientific concepts into value or ethical claims . . . which are, in turn, legitimated by the authority of science" (Buttel: 15). The third tendency is to invoke "alarmism" about the environment to spur political action. As we will note in later discussion, all three of these tendencies have been clearly in evidence as the spotted owl controversy has unfolded.

In drawing implications for rural society of the above developments, Buttel suggests that they have been largely responsible for the replacement of the topic of social justice in public policy debates relating to rural issues by that concerning the environment:

> I cannot help but wonder whether [environmentalism] might over time lead to a fundamental shift in how rural spaces are symbolized, and accordingly how we define and deal with rural problems.

> While the rural tradition in the United States clearly has long had environmental-symbolic elements . . . the strongest and more enduring cultural connotation is one that has seen rural communities and households tending to be underprivileged and worthy of assistance. The establishment . . . of land grant universities and the priority given to rural places and people in the 1960s war on poverty are excellent cases

in point. Many of the positive things we have been able to accomplish in rural America have been premised on this symbolism . . . (Buttel, 1992: 22-23).

He goes on to ask:

What, then, will be the future of rural America if it becomes defined in strong symbolic terms as forest sites or prospective forest acreage needed to curb the greenhouse effect, as pristine ecosystems to ensure clean water for urban use, and as more desirable to the degree that fewer people are there to pollute, disrupt natural habitats, and the like? Will we, in other words, witness a further erosion of commitment to improving the livelihoods of the rural poor and to rural development? Can we think meaningfully of "sustainable development" in nonmetropolitan contexts of the advanced countries (Buttel, 1992: 23)?

In light of these societal changes, the study of Northwestern loggers appears to have implications that extend beyond findings related to this particular group. Loggers are far from the only rural workers whose fortunes have been linked to the trends noted above. Although the events that have occurred in the case of loggers were particularly dramatic, their story may, in some dimensions at least, be the story of most or all rural workers whose jobs are linked to harvesting or extracting and who are caught in global economic change and in the transition of political eras. In view of this, attention in this book will be directed not only to the case studies at its core, but also to the historic evolution of the occupation itself and of the management and the allocation of forest resources upon which it depends.

Policy Context of the Study

Like any group depending directly on the land to make a living, the lives and social organization of loggers have been affected by how various institutions in society (including markets) have structured and regulated the use of the land (Schwantes,1989; Cronon,1991). During the nineteenth century, the timber industry and the logging occupation were migratory, moving , as timber was depleted, from New England through the South, the Lakes States and finally to the Pacific Northwest. In reaction to this migratory pattern and a growing fear that the nation would soon run short of trees to harvest, the Progressive Era conservationists of the turn of the century, with the strong support of President Theodore Roosevelt and led by the first U.S.-born forester, Gifford Pinchot, imported the forestry profession from Europe to the

United States. The Progressives were successful in withdrawing from public entry large segments of forest land (mostly western) and placing it under the jurisdiction of a government agency run by professional foresters. This agency became known as the U.S. Forest Service, and evolved into the largest single public forest land manager in the nation and the trend setter and model for other federal and state agencies to come later (Dana, 1956; Dana and Fairfax, 1980; Clary, 1986).

One of the oft-touted benefits the Progressive visionaries planned to achieve by creating the reserves was the "stabilization" of logging communities previously subject to the migration patterns described above (Dana, 1956; Clary, 1986). In a book written for popular consumption, Pinchot articulated a future vision of the U.S. as a "nation of homes" the materials for which would be provided by the wise, scientifically guided management and use of the country's forest resources (Pinchot, 1972).

Pinchot was instrumental in the development (largely from a mixture of European influences) of forestry as the first natural resource management profession in the U.S. This served the immediate purpose of staffing and administering the reserves with scientifically trained managers (Pinchot, 1967; Hays, 1959). A longer term result was the strong influence in national forest management of what might be termed traditional European forestry. This approach assumed the primacy of wood production over other forest uses, and held as an intermediate objective the large-scale conversion of naturally occurring, ecologically complex woodlands to relatively simple "normal forests", engineered with the idea of sustaining maximum long-term fiber production (Clary, 1986; Behan, 1966, 1991).

The establishment of "government forestry" was only one manifestation of the Progressive's plans for U.S. society, however. Historical scholarship suggests that the designation of the forest reserves was part of the Progressives' larger scheme of creating a more orderly, rationalized society through the positive use of scientific principles applied by trained government experts (Hays, 1959; Lacey, 1979). In Pinchot's words:

> The conservation point of view is valuable in the education of our people as well as in forestry; it applies to the body politic as well as to the earth and its minerals . . . and that is the burden of the message, we are coming to see the logical and inevitable outcome that these principles, which arose in forestry and have their bloom in conservation of natural resources, will have their fruit in the increase and promotion of national efficiency along the lines of national growth (Pinchot, 1967: 49-50).

One aspect of rationalization the orderly minded Progressives seem to have had in mind was what sociologist Norman Hayner was to later call the "Taming of the Lumberjack" from his nomadic frontier ways (Hayner, 1945). Hayner's research indicated that the Northwestern logger of the 1940s was no longer the migrant that his turn of the century logging camp forebearers had been, but rather lived in town and commuted to the woods. The extent to which this change was due to conservation measures versus the further development of technology and the closing of the logging frontier in the lower forty-eight, is a question probably worthy of additional historical analysis. What is clear, as we will discuss in subsequent chapters, is that many of the cultural aspects of the loggers' world have remained remarkably intact in the Northwest.

The post World War II building boom created generally good times for the Northwestern logger. Harvesting technology and safety improved in spite of the perennially cyclic nature of markets for lumber. Demand for forest products was generally strong, and timber supply remained relatively plentiful and accessible. All of these events were an apparent fulfillment the Progressive's vision of "orderly" industrialization through rationalized use of natural resources, the building of a nation of homes, and the creation of a much larger and more prosperous middle class.

However, changes that began to be apparent in the late 1940s were soon to have effects on the logger's world. One of these was a gradual shift in reliance from the private sector to federal lands for trees to harvest. Unlike the Forest Service, the Bureau of Land Management (BLM), and other federal land agencies, most private timber companies were not constrained to practice sustained yield timber management. Most land owning companies harvested or sold timber from their own holdings before looking elsewhere for logs. As private supplies were drawn down, larger companies began to join their smaller non-landowning counterparts in placing greater reliance on public timber to meet the demand while the next generation of trees was maturing on private land (Adams and Haines, 1990).

One historian notes:

The scale and pace of changes in national forest management after the war was truly remarkable. Road construction and logging accelerated at breakneck speed. Under continuous pressure to increase timber harvests, the Forest Service engaged in an unprecedented road-building program to open up more and more backcountry. In this fifteen-year period, approximately 65,000 miles of addititonal roads were bulldozed into national forests . . . . More than half were specifically the timber access roads (Hirt, 1994: XXIII).

Hirt goes on to characterize the harvest levels and federal forest management in the post-war period generally as a product of a "Conspiracy of optimism" about the ability of intensive forest management practices to keep pace with demand for forest products.

During the post World War II period, another development with significance for the future of federal forest management and forest workers was unfolding. This was the emergence of the movement favoring forest preservation into the mainstream of American politics. Although this movement dated back at least as far as John Muir and the battle over flooding the Hetch Hetchy Valley in Yosemite National Park (a dispute that began in the first decade of the century), its advocates had largely confined themselves to advocating the creation and expansion of the national park system and a few, relatively small wilderness areas (Nash, 1967; Wellman, 1987). The movement's growing membership began to respond to increased harvesting and other development activities on public lands by lobbying in favor of wilderness designation for significant acreages of national forest, Bureau of Land Management lands, and other federal holdings. Success was eventually achieved in securing the passage of the Wilderness Act of 1964.

Passage of the 1964 Act, however, was really only the beginning of the serious battles over federal wilderness designation. During the next twenty-five years, the advocates for forest preservation, who also served as a core group in the evolution of the broader environmental movement, devoted an enormous amount of time and energy to administrative and legislative fights concerning specific wilderness set-asides (Stankey, 1989). By the late 1980s, the majority of these battles had reached conclusion (with the notable exception of those concerning federal lands in Idaho, Montana, and Utah) resulting in a national wilderness preservation system comprised largely of lands in high elevation sites and with holdings on a scale far beyond that originally imagined by Aldo Leopold, Robert Marshall, and other early wilderness advocates (Wellman, 1987). These events were instrumental in setting the stage for the next major dispute over federal forest lands, the spotted owl/old-growth battle, as environmentalists now turned attention to the lowland Douglas-fir stands on public lands in western Washington, Oregon, and northern California, which remained in the commercial forest base.

It would be an exaggeration to state that environmentalists concerned with federal land management devoted all of their energies to maximizing the acreage to be included in areas not open to timber and other multiple use management. They were, for example, instrumental in the battles over the practice of clearcutting on commercial forest lands in national forests, most notably in the Bitterroot in Montana and the Monongahela in West Virginia. The latter dispute led to the passage of the National Forest Management Act of 1976 (NFMA), the most far-reaching legislation pertaining to the national forests adopted since 1960 (and arguably since 1905) (Dana and Fairfax, 1981; LeMaster, 1984). This act, technically a series of amendments to the Forest and Range Renewable Resources Planning Act that had been signed into law in 1974 (Dana and Fairfax, 1981; Wilkinson and Anderson, 1987), restructured the process by which national forest planning and decision-making takes place.

Among its many provisions, NFMA limited the size of clear cuts on national forests, specified the timing and rate of restocking of tree seedlings after timber harvest and required consideration of a number of factors including the maintenance of biological diversity and water quality in streams in making land management decisions (Wilkinson and Anderson, 1987). One provision of NFMA was the creation of forest plans, developed on a ten year basis to set the parameters for the management of each national forest. The plans represented an unprecedented opening up of national forest management to public scrutiny. One author described them as a "social contract" between a national forest and its public (Shannon, 1990).

It should be noted, however, that even in the case of NFMA, one of the environmental movement's clear objectives in attempting to influence legislative language was to limit the management discretion of the agency decision makers (most of whom, at that time, were professional foresters in the utilitarian tradition of Pinchot) with whom the environmentalists disagreed philosophically and did not trust to make the kind of changes they sought in federal land management (Hays, 1987).

The environmental movement's major efforts relative to federal forest lands, have continued to focus on protecting land from what its members often view as exploitative management: too focused on commodity production and unduly influenced by industry (Wilkinson, 1992a). The forester's traditional ideal of the "normal forest", structured by age class to provide a sustained yield of timber, is anything but ideal or normal to environmentalists. Unlike the traditional forester, environmentalists are generally concerned with attributes of forests such as biological diversity and the presence of endangered animal and plant species rather than efficient wood production (Drushka, 1992). With the current generation of wilderness battles more or less behind them, and the vast majority of protected wilderness acres in high elevation sites, it was a logical progression for environmental groups to turn attention to the remaining lowland areas of "old-growth" or "ancient" forests that, as it happens, are inhabited by the northern spotted owl.

It should be noted in passing that one ironic turn in the rhetoric of the battle over the federal forests has been the political use of arguments concerning the welfare of forest-based human communities. The Progressive reformers argued that the fate of the communities should not be left to the whims of the industry and the free market, but rather that government land ownership and regulation of timber would serve their long-term interests. In more recent times, advocates for the industry have argued that excessive harvest restrictions on federal lands, influenced by the environmental movement, pose the most significant threat to community stability. In response, some environmental groups have been recently arguing that they favor "sustainable communities", rather than ones based on what they characterize as short term exploitation of forests.

The rise of environmentalism was hardly the only external influence on the Northwestern logger's world, however. For several years in the early 1980s, another event eclipsed timber supply as the major immediate problem facing the timber industry and its employees. This was the most severe and prolonged economic downturn in the forest products economy since the 1930s. Thousands of loggers and millworkers were thrown out of work. As the recession grew worse, many smaller companies went out of business or were absorbed by larger firms. Many timber purchasers defaulted on federal contracts. Hundreds of small independent harvesting operations went bankrupt:

> In the first six months of 1980 more than half of the timber mills in the Douglas-fir belt shut down or curtailed production, laying off or reducing hours of 51,000 workers. Fourteen plywood plants, representing nine percent of the region's productive capacity, announced that they were closing permanently . . . . Aftershocks from these events rippled through the regional economy. One observer noted that the enterprises most "under the gun" . . . [were] independent wood products companies in the Northwest that do not own their own timber but harvest it from private lands [because] aggressive bidding has more than doubled the price they pay for public timber now, compared to five years ago. Unfortunately the tarots had not been reliable (Harbison, 1991: 878).

Proposals and counter proposals over whether to "bail out" floundering timber companies replaced debate over timber supply issues in headlines. Even though relief from federal timber contracts no longer affordable was finally granted (Harbison, 1991), fears that areas of the rural Northwest were fast becoming the "new Appalachia" began to be expressed. The "community stability" issue had taken a decidedly new and painful turn.

By the mid 1980s, the industry was pulling out of the worst of the recession. Forest products was, by description of its own leaders, a changed, more efficient industry that was better equipped to produce efficiently and complete internationally (Bledsoe, 1989). As we noted above, it had lower overhead and fewer employees per unit of output, particularly in the mills. The disadvantage from the point of view of workers of course, was that fewer people were employed.

Not surprisingly, the issue of timber supply and harvest came to the forefront once again. Although a few wilderness designation decisions remained to be made, the controversy centered this time largely on the remaining stands of old-growth trees on public commercial forest land in the Northwest. Lands managed by the Forest Service and the Bureau of Land management were of particular focus. Environmental interests in an attempt to preserve as much of the remaining old-growth mosaic as possible, argued that federal land agencies should choose the northern spotted owl as an "indicator species" for old-growth or ancient forest habitat (Johnston and Krupin, 1991). The owl, as research by wildlife biologists indicated, appears to be largely dependent on old-growth for nesting habitat and survival (Gutierrez, 1985). Consequently, the owl became a symbol in the struggle over the disposition of old-growth forests. Environmentalists fought to have the owl included on the federal threatened and endangered species list under the terms of the Endangered Species Act to ensure protection of its habitat. Industry advocates, many logging community residents and others argued that the fight was about "communities and jobs" versus "owls". Environmentalists and their sympathizers argued that old-growth or ancient forest ecosystems are irreplaceable once they are harvested, and that the industry should speed up its transition to the harvest of second-growth stands and/or reduce the volume of harvest (Morrison, 1988). The industry responded that insufficient volumes of second-growth were available in the short term and that stopping the long planned harvest of old-growth stands would inflict serious damage on the economy of the region, and especially on communities dependent on timber jobs.

Despite the personal intervention of President Clinton beginning in the spring of 1993, the spotted owl controversy has yet to reach anything which might be reasonably called a final resolution. However, the outlines of an outcome seem reasonably clear. Most significant for the current discussion is that it appears to be a *fait accompli* that a significant long-term reduction in the harvest of old-growth forests from previously planned levels will result (Johnston and Krupin, 1991; USDA Forest

Service, 1992; F.E.M.A.T., 1993). A more detailed chronology of events in the spotted owl/old-growth controversy along with a discussion of specific timber and land use policies and events that led up to the current dispute, is provided in Chapter 3. For purposes of this introductory discussion, suffice it to say the owl/old-growth dispute can be seen as but another chapter in the continuing struggle over the disposition and use of forest land in the West, a battle that currently shows little sign of going away (Wilkinson, 1992a). As will be discussed below, this struggle continues to have economic and social consequences for logging and its associated way of life.

Focus of the Book

The central purpose of this volume is to present and provide an interpretation for the results of two sociological field studies that, although separated by both time and space, are closely related in focus; theoretical and methodological approach; and most notably, results. The first study, conducted from 1981 to 1984, was designed to investigate in detail the social organization of loggers in a selected study area in northern California and southern Oregon. In broadest terms, the initial study was an attempt to better understand the way of life of modern day northwestern loggers as one step in developing a more complete picture of the effects of forest land use policies on people in forest based communities (see Lee et al., 1990).

The initial study was not, however, designed specifically as policy research. Rather, the focus was on the sociology of Northwestern loggers. This approach was based on the reasoning that a basic understanding of the lifeways of any group is a necessary prerequisite to drawing inferences about the effects of external influences (such as, in this case, timber supply, regulation, and markets) on such a group. As the study proceeded and regularities in patterns began to emerge in the data, it became increasingly apparent that a number of influences whose individual effects are often very difficult to distinguish from each other were affecting the logger's way of life.

The second study (1991) was commissioned as an assessment of the potential social impacts, in and around three timber communities in western Washington, of sudden timber harvest reductions due to proposed habitat protection for the northern spotted owl. Unlike the first effort that focused exclusively on loggers, the second study was aimed at the full range of people in the study communities who stood to be affected by the harvest reductions. Unless otherwise noted, the discussion in this volume of the results of the second study (particularly those in Chapter 6) focuses specifically on loggers and their immediate families in the two study areas directly affected by the owl issue.

By historical happenstance, the initial study provided vital background and insights, which allowed for the design and conduct of the later study during a time of dramatically heightened uncertainty for loggers. The treatment in this volume is aimed at understanding the effects of the owl/forest issue and related events on members of this occupational group and their families as a (perhaps somewhat extreme) example of the impacts of exogenous social forces on rural workers and their families and communities in a rapidly shifting political economy. In order to grasp the impact of these changes it is helpful to know about the way of life and social organization of those affected. Thus, a considerable portion of this volume is devoted to a description and analysis of what will be termed the Northwestern logger's occupational community.

Study Areas and Approach

It should be noted both studies were conducted in areas west of the Cascade mountains. The technology, and therefore, crew configuration used in logging in this area is somewhat different than that found in the inter-mountain region east of the Cascades where the trees tend to be smaller (Roberge, 1992; Williamson, 1976). It should also be noted, in keeping with long-standing practice in sociological research of this nature, the names and exact locations of the study areas will not be revealed. The primary reason for this is to protect the confidentiality of those observed and interviewed. The site of the initial study encompassed an area of approximately 50 miles in radius near the California-Oregon boarder. The area is largely rural with local employment linked mostly to logging, agriculture, and government service. The local economy had historically been heavily influenced by the cyclic nature of the forest products industry. One feature of the area that made it particularly suitable for the study was the presence of both small independent logging operations and a major land owning timber company that employed its own "company" loggers in some of its harvesting operations?

The fieldwork for the first study was conducted in two phases. A participant observation strategy was adopted for the exploratory phase. The investigator moved to a logging community and, keeping his researcher role very much in the background, sought employment in the woods. He eventually found a job as a choker setter for a gyppo logging contractor. It would be conservative to estimate that a total of 750 hours of active participant observation was conducted during this phase along with six months living in the study area.

The second phase of the first study, begun a year later, consisted of a series of interviews conducted in the study area with loggers and knowledgeable local observers of the logger's world. Following the methodological precepts of "grounded theory" (Glaser and Strauss, 1980; Strauss and Corbin, 1990), interviewees were selected by a process of chain referral and interviews were directed but informal, allowing interviewees to express themselves freely and in their own words on subjects of relevance to the study. The decision to terminate the data gathering was made when novel information ceased to be forthcoming from interviews and the judgment was made by the researcher, in consultation with knowledgeable informants, that the substantively important categories of loggers had been included.

Eighty-one individuals were interviewed over the seven month period that constituted the second phase of the study. The interviews typically ranged from one to three hours, although several lasted considerably longer. A handful of particularly knowledgeable and cooperative "key informants" were revisited on multiple occasions. In some cases interviews were conducted in the home of the interviewee or the investigator, in others they took place on the job. In more than one instance, interviews took place at 2:30 a.m. in the cab of a logging truck on the way to pick up the first load of the day. Several group interviews were also conducted, although every effort was made to follow-up with one-on-one discussions at a later time.

The three areas examined in the second study are all rural and all located in western Washington. The wood products industries in two of the three areas have been heavily linked to old-growth harvesting on public lands in recent years and stood to be severely affected by sudden reductions in available stumpage. The third area in Washington's southwest quadrant has a recent history of dependence on second-growth stands on state and private lands and thus stood to be affected only very indirectly by the owl proposals. The third area was included in the study primarily to attempt to observe any differences in worker or family social organization or characteristics as compared to those in areas feeling the direct effects of the controversy.

All three areas could be characterized as homogeneous with respect to aggregate dependence on forest products or other primary industries. Thus there was little overt evidence of local advocacy for ancient forest preservation and the accompanying intra-community conflict documented in recent research in California (Fortmann and Kusel, 1990). A total of 106 individuals were interviewed in the three areas: twenty-six were loggers, eleven were spouses of loggers; twenty-nine were sawmillworkers, five the spouses of millworkers; sixteen shake and shingle workers, three the spouses of shake and shingle workers; nine local business people; and eighteen community informants (community leaders, officials, teachers etc.). The criteria for selecting interviewees were based on analytic induction (Glaser and Strauss, 1980) and, although across a broader set of categories, nearly identical to those used in the prior study. As was the case in the first study, the interviews lasted from one to three hours with a number of key informants being revisited on several occasions. Another difference between the first and second studies is that in the second, a team of three researchers designed the research, performed the fieldwork and analyzed the results.

Organization of the Book

Chapter 2 discusses the concepts central to the main argument of the book. Most important among these is idea of human community as an entity not necessarily defined by geographic or political boundaries. Chapter 3 is concerned with the historical context of the study. The first portion of the chapter focuses on a discussion of the history and cultural origins of the Northwestern logger. It relies almost entirely on published sources and is included not to be a definitive historical analysis, but rather to provide some context for the current findings. The latter portion of the chapter provides some more specific background on the timber/habitat issue with particular reference to the aspects of these that have affected loggers in the Douglas-fir region.

The next three chapters are a sociological portrait and analysis of the Douglas-fir region logger's lifeways as they were observed and experienced in the course of the fieldwork for the case studies. These are included, as noted above, to provide the reader with a sufficently detailed picture such that the impacts of the owl/old-growth controversy which are described later may be more adequately understood. Chapter 4 is an overview of the social world of the loggers studied. This chapter begins with a brief discussion of the theoretical basis and methodological approach taken in the fieldwork for the studies. Chapter 5 is a treatment of the attributes of the logger's social world. The discussion is organized along the lines of Salaman (1974) and Van Maanen and Barley's (1984) synthesis of other occupational community studies. Chapter 6 treats the strategies would-be loggers use in attempting to gain entry into woods work and how the individuals within the occupation find jobs and gain status. In Chapter 7 attention turns to the impact of the spotted owl/old-growth issue on the Northwestern logger's way of life as observed in the later case study. The book concludes with a chapter concerning social and economic change, land use conflict, and the future of logging and other traditional rural resource based occupations in a dramatically changed policy context.

Notes

1. It is important to point out that the capital substitution for labor question is more complex than this quotation suggests and has become quite controversial, in the wake of the spotted owl issue. Environmentalists have claimed that capital substitution and related economic trends are resulting in employment losses that render job losses due to constrictions of raw material supply in effect, irrelevant because such jobs would have disappeared anyway. The other side argues that restrictions on the supply of commodity resources from public lands are the real cause of such job losses. It is fair to suggest that there is some truth and some hyperbole on both sides of this argument. While there has undoubtedly been substitution of capital for labor in most if not all sectors of the industry, recent work by Greber (1993) and Conway and Wells (1994) suggest that some of the recent media coverage of these trends has overstated them. Greber's analysis concludes, for example, that in the Pacific Northwest, wood products employment per unit of output increased during the 1970s, decreased in the early 1980s and began to increase once again in the late 1980s. Greber forcasts stable to increasing labor per unit of output during the 1990s. Conway and Wells report that in Oregon, lumber wood products employment fluctuated between 70,000 and 80,000 jobs from 1945 to 1980, with the recession and restructuring in the early 80's dropping employment to 55,000, with an increase to 70,000 by 1988. They go on to note that employment has dropped sharply since 1988, coinciding with harvest restrictions related to the spotted owl/old growth controversy. If there is any consensus in the literature concerning this issue, it is that capital replacement of labor has tended to occur sporadically at particular points in history rather than gradually and systematically over time.

2

Community as an Idea:
A Conceptual Issue with Practical
Implications

During the period from the rise of the Progressive movement through the 1960s a strong connection was drawn both in public deliberations and policy formation between forest management and regulation and rural economic development and stability (Pinchot, 1972 ed; Clary, 1986). An example of this is found in Dana (1956):

> Recognition of the fact that the stability of certain communities dependent primarily on the manufacture of forest products can be assured only by the steady and continuous flow of raw materials from the forest led Congress to pass the sustained yield forest management act of March 29, 1944 (Dana, 1956: 284).

This theme was part of a larger societal consensus throughout most of the first half of the present century that the promotion of rural community welfare was a worthy undertaking and one that the government should promote (Buttel, 1992). Consequently, discussions concerning the social consequences of forest resource management decisions for those employed in logging and other forms of resource extraction have usually been framed in terms of human communities and their stability (Society of American Foresters, 1989).

Determining the nature of community in general, as well as the effect of the community in the interactions of loggers, can become a confusing and frustrating enterprise. In sociological literature there is not a consensus on even so much as a definition of community. For example, one of the best known researchers in the community field, George Hillery, identified ninety-four separate definitions in the literature (1982).

Without delving into all the complexity of this literature, the thinking of the social historian Thomas Bender, is particularly useful in understanding the problem at hand. Building on the work of community theorist, Robert Nisbit (1962), Bender (1978) rejects the notion that communities are necessarily territorially bound entities, but instead offers a social-psychological view of community that takes into account the notion of self or identity:

> A community involves a limited number of people in a somewhat restricted social space or network held together by shared understandings and a sense of obligation. Relationships are close, often intimate, and usually face to face. Individuals are bound together by affective or emotional ties rather than by a perception of individual self-interest. There is a "we-ness" in a community; one is a member. Sense of self and of community may be difficult to distinguish . . . .
> Communal relationships are diffuse in their concerns. They are not segmented relationships, and they are not oriented to narrow or specific ends. While a community is part of broader social aggregates, it remains a distinct social grouping. Far from being a microcosm of the whole society, it has a special quality that may result in tension with larger social aggregates. One's network of community, although it may not supply all the warmth and emotional support one needs, is an elemental fact of one's emotional life (Bender, 1978: 7-8).

Thus the idea of community adopted in this study is one of network and identity rather than that of a territorially bounded aggregation of people. This is not to say that geography is not a factor in community dynamics. This view treats geography or territoriality as a variable rather than a constant; people who reside side by side may or may not share enough in common to be members of the same community. Instead, people may be members of multiple communities from which identity and emotional sustenance is drawn. As Ellis notes in her study of Chesapeake fishing communities:

> Eventually, it became clear that geography alone was not enough to locate Fishneck as a community. Common kinpeople as well as common space formed the community boundaries (Ellis, 1986: 10.)

While this point may seem excessively academic to the practical-minded reader, it should be pointed out that it does lead one to ask questions that may have very practical import. For example, in Chapter 7 the finding that various groups of residents of the same towns were affected very differently by the owl crisis will be analyzed. In thinking about "community impacts" of outside forces, it is important to look both at geographic communities and those whose social boundaries do not necessarily correspond to town or city limits.

Territorial Community and the Forest Base

In discussing the controversy in the sociological literature over "territorial" versus "non-territorial" notions of community, Kenneth Wilkinson points to a flaw in the reasoning of those who argue that territory no longer matters:

> The most obvious flaw is in rejecting the simple fact that most people, past and present, live and move and have most of their being in everyday life in local settlements. This is true even though extensive contacts occur among people in different settlements and even though much of the social life in any settlement has little to do with the locality. . . .
>
> If the essence of community is a natural process of social interaction, as assumed here, there is little doubt that community can occur in local settlements where people interact with each other daily. The local territory, therefore, is the logical place to begin the search for community, even if the study takes one beyond the locality as well (Wilkinson, 1991: 22-23).

The seminal early research conducted concerning the relationships of human communities (seen as territorially based entities) to the management of forests in the western U.S. was work carried out in the 1940's by Harold and Lois Kaufman (1990 edition). Not surprisingly, their work was built around the Progressive Era notion of seeking ways to stabilize communities. However, the Kaufmans went beyond Progressive Era thinking of rural society as essentially static. Rather, they defined community stability as a condition of "orderly change". The Kaufmans advocated a multi-step approach to stabilizing a forest dependent community. Their approach, conceived decades ago, has a strikingly current flavor. It called for a stable timber industry, a diversified and balanced economy, effective local leadership, good education, effective community organization, comprehensive forest management planning and local involvement in forest decision-making. Unfortunately, in the thirty-five years following the Kaufman's work, little further sociological attention was devoted to forest communities in the U.S.

During the 1980s, sociologists began to renew their interest in U.S. forest communities. Building on the theorizing of Walter Firey and others, Robert Lee (1982, 1984, 1990) challenged the then prevailing view among forest economists that there is no link between sustained yield forest management and the stability of communities. In developing his argument, he suggested that the relationships between forests and communities can be more completely understood by examining social institutions, rather than simply focusing on individual behavior in the market place. Robert Muth (1990) followed up on this reasoning in examining subsistence resource use by local residents in southeast Alaska. He concluded that, although subsistence use (mandated by federal and state law) is undergoing significant "transformation" in the state, its continued existence is dependent on resource availability, specialized knowledge of harvesters, and a regulatory environment that supports its continuation. He points out that all three requirements are predicated on institutional continuity.

Until recently, most discussions of forest-human community relationships have been largely focused on a single resource -- generally timber. However, Machlis and Force (1988) suggest a broader, more environmental approach to community stability. They call for measures of persistence, constancy, resilience and adaptation in trying to measure stability. They also suggest examining the specific role of resource extraction and use (i.e., timber harvesting and processing, mineral production, etc.) on social change in communities.

In following up on the latter suggestion, Machlis and colleagues attempted to measure the impact of historical changes in resource production rates (minerals and timber) for periods of up to sixty-five years in two Idaho communities. In describing complex and somewhat contradictory findings, the authors state: "Ironically, while the hypothesis was supported, the causal image is blurred by the results. The relationship between resource production and social change is far from clear" (Machlis, Force, and Balice, 1990: 421). A follow-up study, looking specifically at the relationships between rates of timber production over various time periods and social change variables, yielded similar results (Force, Machlis, Zhang, and Kearney, 1993).

However, another perspective on the relationship of changes in timber harvest levels to the well being of forest based communities is provided by a team of analysts who focused on local economies in Idaho. Their study concluded:

> Communities of the west-central Idaho highlands would do well to consider a reduction in the timber harvest, and its implications for their economic future. As we have seen, it is not simply a matter of lost jobs in the timber industry itself. Other jobs and income in the timber-linked business and consumer support industries, as well as in local

government, are tied to timber as well. If there is a timber harvest reduction, communities will either replace lost income with other industry, perhaps tourism, or their economies will have to contract (Robison, et al., 1989: 22).

The issue of social and economic stability (and particularly instability) in rural communities has been the subject of sociological attention across a wide variety of natural resource settings. The general tone of the literature on this subject has been anything but upbeat. A recent review of this literature (Krannich and Luloff, 1991) states:

> The problems of instability associated with cyclical growth, stagnation and decline appear to be particularly pervasive in communities which are resource dependent, e.g., where economic social and cultural conditions of community life are intertwined with . . . the production of a natural resource commodity or commodities . . . Patterns of resource dependence emerge in a variety of settings, but primarily involve communities in which economic activity revolves around agriculture, forestry, fisheries, mining, petroleum resource development and recreation and tourism attractions . . . (Krannich and Luloff, 1991: 7).

Among the problems noted are instability of employment linked to the seasonality and the economic boom and bust cycles of many natural resource industries, patterns of dramatic in and out migration and the draining away of "human capital" (i.e., younger, highly trained people) during periods of out migration (Krannich and Luloff, 1991). The authors note that many of these problems are rooted in the fact that the economic fate of many such communities is often in the hands of corporate entities whose headquarters are located at great distances from the locations where the consequences of their decisions will be felt. As discussed further in a later chapter, the spotted owl controversy is in many ways, an example of this pattern with the added complication that the "extra-local interests" are not just corporate, but also political groups located, in many cases, far from the impacts of the decisions. Another difference we will discuss in the case of the spotted owl issue is that many of the workers most dramatically affected are employees and owners of small, family owned forest products operations depending upon federal timber, while many larger, land owning timber companies stand to benefit from harvest restrictions on federal lands.

Another difficulty well documented in the literature on natural resource- based communities, is conflict over incompatible resource uses and values. Krannich and Luloff state:

One major consequence of this incompatibility is the potential for widespread community conflict between those who espouse established and traditional resource-dependent activities and those wishing to promote new resource utilization processes and activities. Many resource-dependent communities exhibit social and cultural systems which have evolved over the course of generations that are intricately intertwined with the traditional . . . economic structures of resource utilization. [Such] social and cultural systems can limit local acceptance of development options that are perceived to clash with the established . . . community social organization (Krannich and Luloff, 1991: 11-12).

Other recent research suggests that, in some cases, the roots of resource conflicts are more complex than simply "old-timers versus newcomers." Work by Blahna (1990) in Michigan and Fortmann and Kusel in California, (1990) suggests that, in some cases, alliances may form between some newcomers and some old-timers to "give voice" to perspectives that have been long, but "silently," held by some long time community residents. More recent work by Brandenburg (1994) discusses cultural differences between 1970s "back to the land" rural immigrants and more recent urban-to-rural immigrants who have less "hands on" attachment to the land. The latter analysis suggests that, although the "back to the land" types are more environmentalist in a global sense than traditional rural people, part of their motivation for moving to rural areas was an admiration for traditional culture. This is in contrast to the more recent rural immigrants, who tend to see traditional rural culture as simply exploitive of the environment.

Moving Beyond the Territorial Community

As we noted above, if territoriality is accepted as a variable, rather than a constant, in one's view of community, it allows for the casting of a broader net in the "search for community." Along with some of the groupings briefly noted in the paragraphs above, the area of occupations appears useful to look at in the current context. Within the discipline of sociology, there is a rich tradition of the study of occupational groups. The literature most pertinent to the current study is concerned with occupational communities. The central notion of this literature is that, rather than simply being a way to make a living, work in some occupations may become a major focus of the individual's "on" and "off" duty life. Members of occupational communities are a group possessing some degree of a common life and who see themselves as set apart from others in society (Salaman, 1974). Van Maanen and Barley (1984) suggest a definition of occupational community with four components: people who view themselves to involved in the same sort of work, whose identity is closely linked to that work, who share "values, norms, and perspectives" connected to, but extending beyond, the work setting and whose networks of social relationships "meld the realms of work and leisure."

The authors state:

> Occupational communities . . . create and sustain relatively unique work cultures consisting of, among other things, task rituals, standards for proper and improper behavior, work codes surrounding relatively routine practices, and for the membership at least, compelling accounts attesting to the logic and value of these rituals, standards and codes. We suggest that the quest for occupational self control provides the special motive for the development of occupational communities (Van Maanen and Barley, 1984: 287).

The literature on occupational communities is quite extensive, although British sociologists have historically been somewhat more active in this area than their American counterparts. Among the British contributions to the occupational community literature are Banton's (1964) and Fielding's (1986) work on police, Brown and Brennen's study of shipbuilders (1970a and b), Horobin (1957), Turnstall's (1962) studies of fisherman, the work of Dennis, et al. (1956), and Moore (1975) on coal miners, Sykes' (1969a and b) work on navvies (construction workers), Cannon's (1967) study of compositors, Hollowell's (1968) book on lorry (truck) drivers, and Salaman's (1971, 1974) studies of railway men and architects. North American work in this area includes Lipsit et al. (1956) famous study of printers, Becker's (1963) work on jazz musicians, Janowitz's (1960) study of soldiers, Reimer's (1977) work on electricians, Miller and Johnson's (1981) study of Alaskan salmon fishermen, Pollnac and Poggie's (1988) work on New England fishermen and Davis's (1986) work on the spouses of Newfoundland fishermen. Particularly relevant to this volume is Williamson's (1976) anthropological study of independent, "gyppo" loggers in northern Idaho.

The notion that an individual's self or identity can be linked to a particular occupation is certainly not a new idea in sociology. For example, Everett C. Hughes apparently coined the term "occupational self" in his pioneering work in the sociology of occupations (1958 edition). The concept was also present in much of the classic work carried out over the years by Howard Becker (Becker, 1951; Becker and Carper, 1956; Becker and Strauss, 1956; Becker, 1963). An individual with a strong occupational identity has a strong emotional commitment to the occupation and tends to identify him or herself with the occupational role:

Members of such communities will not only see themselves in terms of their occupational role, they will also value this self-image. This process is unlikely to occur among people who are in occupations that do not have occupational communities, and it is extremely unlikely among those workers who have an instrumental orientation towards their work and who wish to escape totally from their work once they leave the work place (Salaman, 1974: 22-23).

A good example of a strong occupational self (in this case among miners) is found in the following:

Somehow, when you get into mining and if you like the men you work with, you just get to the place after a while that you don't want to leave. Once that fever gets hold of a man, he'll never be good for anything else . . . A fellow may quit the mines, but when they whistle he goes back. . . . (Friedmann and Havinghurst, 1954: 70-71)

The notion that an individual has a strong occupational self means that the occupational role identity -- fisherman, miner, logger -- assumes a place of prominence in the set of role identities that individuals carry around as a normal product of socialization (McCall and Simmons, 1978). It does not imply that the occupational role identity is the only item in the member's repertoire. It does suggest that the occupational role identity is very prominent in terms of overall self image and tends to be central in the presentation of self to others (particularly to outsiders). It also tends to be the case that role identities defined within the relevant social milieu and that conflict with the occupation are not likely to be found. Thus a "die-hard" member of the AFL-CIO is not likely to identify with the Republican party, nor, as we shall see, is the typical "gyppo" logger likely to identify himself as a sympathizer with the Sierra Club. Van Maanen and Barley state:

Without question, social identities are sensitive to and reflective of the social situations to which an individual is party. But, for members of occupational communities at least, occupational identities are typically presented to others with some pride and are not identities easily discarded, for they are central to an individual's self image.

Indirect evidence of identification with an occupation is demonstrated by distinctive accouterments, costumes and jargon. Members of fishing communities wear particular types of baseball caps to tell other fishermen what port they are from and what their involvement with fishing is likely to be . . . Police officers carry courtesy cards, off duty revolvers, and wallet badges. The unique properties of each convey significant clues to other officers as to where the owner stands in the community . . . Electricians recognize other electricians by the color of their overalls and by the shoes they wear (Van Maanen and Barley, 1984: 299).

As we noted above, another feature of occupational communities is that the member tends to rely on others within the occupation in developing and then reinforcing his or her self image. Perhaps the most extreme example of this in the literature is Becker's jazz musicians who were found to reject most conventions of non members (squares) and look only to each other (cats) for reinforcement.

> I have noted that musicians extend their desire for freedom from outside interference in their work to a generalized feeling that they should not be bound by the ordinary conventions of their society. The ethos of the profession fosters an admiration for the spontaneous and individualistic behavior and a disregard for the rules of society in general . . . One point of contact is on the job where the audience is the source of trouble . . . Another area of contact is the family. Membership in family binds the musician to people who are squares, outsiders who abide by social conventions, whose authority the musician does not acknowledge (Becker, 1963: 114).

Van Maanen and Barley also note that the more "pervasive, esoteric and numerous the codes" used by occupation members to interpret events, the more likely the occupation is to influence identity. This is due to the influence of such codes on the individual's perception of reality which override a "lay" interpretation. Thus the off-duty mechanic is ever alert to engine malfunction and the vacationing police officer to indications of criminal wrongdoing.

Membership in an occupational community is also marked by high levels of involvement in work and notably, its symbolic attributes. This leads to a sense of "we" and "they," not only with respect to those outside the line of work, but also regarding those who pursue or interpret the meaning of the work differently. An example is the historic rivalry among branches of the U.S. military. Other attributes that tend to build involvement in and identification with an occupation include danger, the belief that one possesses rare, valued or esoteric skills, and the sense that one is responsible for the well being of others, thus leading to the "perception that oneself and one's colleagues are somehow different from the rest of the working population" (Van Maanen and Barley, 1984: 302).

One result of the reliance of occupational community members upon each other for reinforcement of self conceptions and common attitudes, values, and norms, is a set of shared meanings, or to use other language, a social reality unique in some ways to the group. (Berger and

Luckmann, 1967). Van Maanen and Barley (1984) note that the visible indications of occupational community membership or "tie signs" serve as the most obvious links in a complex combination of codes through which members communicate to each other "an occupationally specific view of their work world." This unique social world typically also includes a specialized language, as well as agreed upon definitions of significant social objects. Becker's jazz musicians, for example, defined their music as esoteric art, rather than primarily as a source of entertainment for their audience.

The reference group serves to create shared meanings with respect to: " . . . moral standards surrounding what work is considered good and bad, what work is 'real work' and, therefore, in contrast to 'shit work' what formal and contextual rules of conduct are to be enforced, what linguistic categories are to be used in partitioning the world, and so forth" (Van Maanen and Barley, 1984: 303). Among the conditions that lead to the adoption of occupation-based shared values are a sense that the occupation is stigmatized by the larger society (thus forcing members to turn inward for support), occupations that, for any of a variety of reasons, cut across multiple aspects of the individual's life (i.e., occupation-based standards of behavior that extend beyond the job or responsibilities that do not permit one to be completely off duty) and occupations that entail demanding socialization to attain membership (Salaman, 1974; Van Maanen and Barley, 1984).

The final characteristic of occupational communities noted above is that, for members, work and non-work social relationships are not entirely separable, but tend to overlap and converge. Work relationships are incorporated into the individual's personal life. Off-duty relationships tend to be formed with work friends. In some cases, this is partly due to the unusual schedules of some occupational groups. The Hull fishermen studied by Turnstall (1969) for example, were at sea for long periods of time. When they returned to shore, they used a significant portion of their time to socialize with other fishermen in bars. Many of the printers studied by Lipset et al. (1956) worked nights and found their schedules to be "out of sync" with those of their families. Thus, they tended to engage in spare time activities with their occupational peers. Williamson 1976) states that the northern Idaho gyppo loggers fit this pattern:

> The irregular work regime that [loggers] follow severely limits the time they have for participation in and commitment to structured activities and events in the community. During the three or four months of the busy work season, when work continues from sunrise to sunset, and when most weekends are spent repairing and maintaining equipment,

there is little time for anything other than irregular visits with kinsmen and work friends, either in taverns, homes, or at mill yards and repair shops during the course of work.

During the winter months, when work may cease altogether, the pattern of home visits, tavern drinking, and informal interactions in the community intensifies somewhat . . . In most cases, the networks of kinsmen and friends involved in these non-work activities closely resemble those involved in work related activities (Williamson, 1976: 124-125).

Van Maanen and Barley note that another characteristic of occupations which tends to foster occupational community dynamics is that membership is linked to kinship (1984). The convergence of on and off-duty social networks is not, however, always due to duty schedules or other structural characteristics of work. Individuals who focus their lives on work and who develop common perspectives and interests often tend, quite simply, to be more comfortable in the company of others who share their occupationally specific world view.

At the beginning of the first study, the ideas found in the occupational community literature seemed to describe the Northwestern loggers' way of life. Initially, the research was focused on the question of whether Northwestern loggers (specifically those west of the Cascades) can be accurately described as an occupational community. A second related task (assuming the answer to the first question was "yes") was to explore the implications of the existence of such an occupational community for the logger's ability to adapt to changes both in economic conditions and in the way public forests are managed. As will be suggested in later chapters, the answer to the first question, based on the evidence gathered in these studies is a clear "yes" and its consequences have proven to be both more complex and dramatic than initially anticipated. These issues will be revisited following a discussion of the results of the study.

Thinking beyond the owl/old-growth controversy, one of the hoped for results of the publication of this volume is a heightened interest among natural resource and rural sociologists in the concept of occupational community. The notion seems very useful in understanding patterns of continuity and change among a variety of rural workers in an era in which many are threatened with a loss of occupational self control and as a result, face significant changes in long established ways of life.

3

The Historical Context

Notes on Logging's History in the United States

Stewart Holbrook, rightfully accorded the status as the most popular (not to mention the most colorful) of the North American logging historians (Lucia, 1975), traces the differentiation of logging as a distinct occupation to northern New England in about 1800:

> No man can say just when the species logger appeared. The early American hewers and sawyers of wood were called "lumberers," whether they worked in the forest or in the sawmill. Most of them did both, cutting the forest into logs during the winter, and in summer sawing the laws into boards. Yet the professional logger, the man who would work in the woods or at nothing at all was sighted as early as 1801 by E. A. Kendall, a visiting Englishman (Holbrook, 1938: 41).

The historian goes on to quote the Englishman's rather horrified account of the wild, hard drinking ways of this "species" of men. Holbrook then states:

> But the dismal picture though it be, and one-sided, Mr. Kendall's description of the logger was accurate enough in 1801 or in 1901. What the Englishman did not see was that the life of the logger would in a single generation or so produce a race of men who in the large didn't give a tinker's damn for property; and who were as hardy a race of men as ever walked. Natural selection by forthright elimination would do it. (Holbrook, 1938: 42)

It is perhaps ironic that this rough and ready occupational group "evolved" in the region of the country whose residents have been generally known for their proper and thrifty lifeways. One can only wonder at the reaction of "proper New Englanders" to the loggers' custom of coming into town after a log drive to "blow her in".

As we will note in later chapters, the ethos of logging (as opposed to forestry) involved thinking in the short term with little or no thought about replanting trees, or for that matter saving money beyond the next trip to town. The logger saw his job as "letting daylight into the swamp" and moving on to a new swamp. Indeed, this ethos can be seen to be quite rational in the sense that the economy of rural New England was to be based for more than a century on agriculture, and trees stood quite literally in the way of most agricultural activities (Raup, 1966). In addition, there were many trees to be harvested to the west.

Farming was not attractive to the typical New England logger, so when the swamps of New England had more daylight than merchantable trees, primarily white pine since spruce was considered next to worthless, it was time for the logger and his industry to move on. New England was to experience another logging boom in the first decade of the new century when spruce became valuable, but by that time the pioneering loggers were cutting Douglas-fir in the Northwest.

Holbrook (1938) reports that the migration to the Midwest began in 1836 when a lumberman from Maine purchased timberlands on the St. Clair River in Michigan. A new sawmill town, Augusta, was founded by former residents of its namesake in Maine. The migration continued into the Civil War years. The logging migration largely leapfrogged over the Middle Atlantic states, although Pennsylvania provided some logging employment for migrating Maine loggers. By the time of the great migration, however, most of the pine in Pennsylvania had been harvested by native Pennsylvania Dutch, Irish, Germans, and a handful of French Canadians. Despite that, Pennsylvania is notable as the site of the first significant logger unrest in the industry. In the early 1870s, millworkers responded to a "speed up" order from mill owners in Williamsport with a strike. Holbrook reports that although strikebreakers hired by the operators were ultimately successful, loggers came down from the hills to join in the melee" and got in more excellent fighting than they had seen in a decade of barroom assaults." (1938: 80) Labor unrest was to be more serious, and of greater consequence, in the Lake states and especially in the Northwest.

By the 1860s, Saginaw, Michigan, had replaced Bangor as the lumbering capitol of North America. By this time, steam-powered sawmills were in operation, the output from which dwarfed anything Maine could claim in its first logging heyday. At one point in the 1880s, 112 sawmills operated along the Saginaw River. In 1882, a reported 1.012 billion board feet of lumber was provided there along with 300 million shingles. Ten years later, most of its mills had closed as the wave of logging swept westward (Holbrook, 1938).

Not everyone was as sanguine about the situation as the logger-historian, however. A committee was appointed in 1869 by the Michigan legislature to look into the question of "forest destruction". An excerpt of their report as chronicled by Dana (1956) stated:

> The interests to be subserved, and the evils to be avoided by our action on this subject have reference not alone to this year or the next score of years, but generations yet unborn will bless or curse our memory according as we preserve for them what the munificent past has so richly bestowed upon us, or as we lend our influence to continue and accelerate the wasteful destruction everywhere at work in our beautiful state. (Dana, 1956: 77)

Nonetheless, the loggers followed the receding line of trees from lower Michigan to the Upper Peninsula to Wisconsin and northern Minnesota. During this period, logging technology evolved, particularly in the sawmill, with the invention of the headsaw and the bull chain for moving logs more efficiently from the log ponds to the mill. Mill ponds were now heated in the winter with steam, thus ensuring year round operation of mills.

Mill innovation resulted in increased pressure in the woods. Woods operations responded with the replacement of oxen with horses and the invention of big wheels to ease log skidding over stumps, thus freeing loggers from their dependence on snow. In 1886, Horace Butters, a former Maine logger, patented the first version of the mechanical skidder powered by two steam engines. Although his invention was not adopted in the Lake states, its successors were to revolutionize logging in the South and especially in the West. Also in the 1880s, the crosscut saw, later known as the misery whip, came into use for falling, while the axe was relegated to notching undercuts and limbing (Holbrook, 1938).

Holbrook reports that labor organization had never been taken seriously by early loggers:

> Loggers of the Great Days were as willing to work as horses. They took pride in the quality of their work and even more in the quantity. Canny foremen kept this spirit keen by pitting crews against each other and by offering small bonuses. The best foremen often were those who could fell a tree or break a jam faster than anybody else--and of course lick any man in the crew (Holbrook, 1938: 105).

However, in the autumn of 1881 workers of the Muskegon Booming Association at Muskegan, Michigan struck, demanding a ten-hour day. Troops were brought in. The strike fizzled, but re-erupted in the spring, at which point the operators brought in Pinkerton "detectives". The result was that the men went back to work on a ten-hour basis (Holbrook, 1938). On the subject of labor organizing in the Lake states, the historian concluded that Lake States loggers cared less about hours worked in the woods and more about the quality of entertainment to be found in town when the log drive was over.

As the Lake states timber supply was drawn down, the so called "second migration" of loggers began:

> Eager to sell land and generate freight, the railroads in turn sponsored excursions of investors to the Pacific Northwest.

> Two things were especially impressive about the timber of western Washington: it grew in heavy stands and it was cheap. In the Great Lakes states, merchantable timber averaged 6,600 feet per acre, a fifth of the rate on the coast. The average value of standing timber in 1890, moreover, was 92 cents per thousand feet in Washington, compared to $3.26 on the Great Lakes. High-quality stands could be purchased for as little as 10 cents per thousand feet. These figures were readily translated into greatly reduced costs of operation. A third of the cost of manufacturing lumber in the [L]ake [S]tates consisted of stumpage, but only eleven percent on the Pacific coast. Declining supply in the east, vast supply in the west, and the railroad connection made for an influx of lumbermen (Ficken, 1987: 59).

Holbrook (1938) estimates that about a quarter of the Lake states loggers went to the south to cut southern pine, while the "main army" traveled to the Northwest to harvest Douglas-fir. The major portion of the migration took place in the 1880s and 1890s, and by 1905 the state of Washington was leading the country in lumber production (Ficken, 1987). However, conditions that the lumbermen and loggers faced in the Northwest forced some changes in tactics relative to harvesting and transporting logs. The main problem faced was the sheer size and mass of the trees to be harvested.

> Who felled the first big fir is not known, but perhaps the earliest picture of an authentic blown-in-the-bottle logger at work concerns one Clement Adams Bradbury. Even the place, the date, and the time of day when the pioneer logger performed are known.

> Shortly after noon on the fifteenth day of January 1847, Logger Bradbury, fresh from York County, Maine, stepped up to a mighty old

fir that grew by the Columbia River some twenty miles east of Astoria, Oregon, and hard by the new sawmill of W. H. H. Hunt. He observed the tree's butt, which was eight feet in diameter, and he looked upward with something of awe to a top that seemed near the clouds. There had been no such stuff on the Saco Down East (Holbrook, 1938: 162-163).

Holbrook reports that Bradbury "felled" the tree but not before he had been doused with a "copious flow" of pitch, which caused him to wait until the next day to finish his work.

However, felling was actually the least of the loggers' problems. Transporting the fallen logs presented far more formidable difficulties that necessitated several innovations in logging practices. The first, and what Holbrook refers to as the "Western loggers' . . . greatest contribution to the science of moving timber," was the use of the skidroad. This fairly simple innovation involved clearing a path either to a mill site or a watercourse and felling or placing smaller trees with limbs removed across the path to serve as skids to reduce friction as mill bound logs were pulled across them. Due to the weight of the logs to be "skidded", western loggers quickly abandoned the horses that had been used in the later years in Maine and in the Lake states and returned to the use of oxen, referred to as bulls. Holbrook points out that this innovation led to an addition to the status hierarchy in the woods:

> By all odds the most important man of a woods crew in the bull-team era was the bullwacker. He was paid three times as much as an axeman, and his opinions on all subjects from oxshoes to the cosmos were considered weighty. He ruled the skidroad, man and beast, with a firm and practiced hand, and his badge of authority was his goadstick, a slim piece of wood some five feet long with a steel brad in one end (1938: 165).

The age of the bull wacker was not to last long in the woods of the Northwest, however. In 1881 a logger/inventor from Eureka California, John Dolbeer, built the first steam "donkey" for skidding logs, thus ushering in the steam era of western logging:

> It was the dawn of a new age, and no one could envision the changes. The donkey and ground lead system increased the volume of the cut and the output of the mills. The trees came down that much faster. In turn, logging operators and sawmill men increased their payrolls many times over. At the same time logging operators were eyeing the railroads with all that great locomotive power, although the kind of railroading done on the mainlines was far too fancy for the rugged forests. The woods were now on the verge of a machine revolution and

the next few years would see the greatest changes since Jamestown (Lucia, 1975: 17-18).

Changes in technology were accompanied by changes in the relationships between workers and employers. In earlier times, owners felt some affinity for their employees, but by the 1880s had adapted a more impersonal attitude, particularly when the workforce was no longer dominated by fellow New Englanders:

> Lumbermen referred to wages as the "price of labor" in much the same fashion as they would discuss the cost of logs and animals. When production cutbacks were instituted, no thought was given to the impact of reduced earnings or employees and their families. Rather than acknowledging the contribution of workers, lumbermen treated them with scorn. "We appreciate the position you are in," Will Talbot sympathized with Cyrus Walker on one occasion, "in having to deal with such a poor class of labor" (Ficken, 1987: 72-73).

The first skirmish between organized labor and timber operators in the Northwest involved the Knights of Labor in 1885. The first objective of the Knights was the expulsion of inexpensive Chinese labor from mills in the Puget Sound region. Some mills bowed to pressure and fired their Chinese workers, others did not. This incident was followed by a successful campaign by the Knights to institute a ten (as opposed to twelve) hour day in the Puget Sound mills. The episode hardened the attitudes of employers toward unions and workers, and helped to set the stage for later, more serious confrontations with labor.

> What was needed according to Cyrus Walker, was a return to the old days when mill owners were treated with deference . . . In common with American businessmen of the time, Northwest lumbermen defended their right to form combinations, but denied to labor the right to organize in defense of its interests. They were willing to pay high wages and to improve conditions of labor, but were unwilling to concede the legitimacy of unions (Ficken, 1987: 75).

As the century drew to a close, logging technology continued to rapidly evolve. Ground lead logging gave way to high lead logging in which a chosen "spar tree" was topped by a high climber, and then guyed up with steep cables and a block attached through which a cable connected to a donkey engine was run. This arrangement allowed for lifting an end of the log off the ground for fast retrieval. The system became known as "highballing". Holbrook (1938) noted that the high lead system nearly doubled logging production but also greatly increased accident rates. Andrew Prouty (1982) in a dissertation entitled *More Deadly than War* noted that an average of one worker per day was killed in the woods of the Northwest during the steam logging era.

Another very significant technological development was the development by John Shay of a geared steam locomotive for logging:

> The timberman slapped rails back into the wilderness without knowledge that it couldn't be done. . . . All rules for accepted railroading were broken and new tracks blazed piecemeal with scanty regulations. The railroads became the lifeblood of the industry, the leader in one of several revolutions to eliminate muscle power from the woods. In time the logging highball became synonymous with the railroad highball, from which the term originated. Both were easily the most dangerous work in the world (Lucia, 1975: 22).

As the harvesting and transportation technology changed, it became far more expensive to run a logging operation. Smaller logging operators were eliminated from competition, and human and animal power were replaced by machinery, thus shifting the balance of economic power in favor of large corporations (Lucia, 1975). These developments set the stage for a period of significant labor organization and unrest led in large part by the Industrial Workers of the World (IWW), commonly known as the Wobblies:

> Mention has been made of religious bands and soapbox orators of the skidroads. The Christian evangelists made little headway among loggers; nor did rousers for the Knights of Labor, the Populists nor the Socialists. Loggers might grumble about low wages or poor living conditions in the camps, but they did nothing about them until a smoldering ember of Karl Marx set fire to their tails. It was the Wobblies who blew spark into the flame (Holbrook, 1938: 207).

The IWW was organized in 1904 in Chicago in large part by the man who became its general secretary, W. D. (Big Bill) Haywood. Although there were no loggers present at the original organizational meeting, the movement quickly began to pick membership in logging camps throughout the West. The event that created untold amounts of publicity to the movement was the indictment and subsequent acquittal of Haywood and another labor organizer in the bombing murder of Frank Steunenberg, former governor of Idaho. President Theodore Roosevelt came out publicly against Haywood and his colleagues as "undesirable citizens" and Northwestern loggers began to wear buttons reading, "I am an undesirable citizen" (Holbrook, 1938).

Like many social movements, the rise of the influence of the Wobblies among loggers and millworkers was meteoric. The first strike took place in Portland in 1907. Although the strike was quickly broken, it gained the movement many adherents. This was followed by a "free speech" battle in Spokane, led in part by a fiery woman IWW organizer, Elizabeth Gurky Flynn. When Spokane police jailed Flynn, the resulting demonstrations heavily sprinkled with caulked booted loggers frightened Spokane authorities into releasing jailed "Wobs" and allowing them the "soapbox" in the city (Holbrook, 1938). In 1908, loggers dominated the IWW convention in Chicago, forming the "Overall Brigade" and calling for strikes and sabotage rather than political activity as a means of achieving control of the sources of industrial production (Holbrook, 1954). Many strikes, most of them short lived, followed. In November, 1916, the most famous Wobbly incident known as the "Everett Massacre" took place. A chartered steamer with approximately 400 Wobblies aboard docked in that part of town and were soon caught up in a shooting battle that left seven people dead and scores wounded (Ficken, 1987).

In 1917 in the midst of the first World War, the Wobblies called the largest strike in history against the Northwest timber operators, demanding an eight-hour day and better working conditions and living conditions in camp. The specific events of the strike, which involved approximately eighty-five percent of the logging camps and mills in the region, are too numerous and involved to detail here. The ultimate result was the intervention by the federal government, which saw as its overriding interest the maintenance of the production of spruce to build airplanes for the war effort. The intervention was in the form of the appointment of Colonel Brice P. Disque, whose charge was to resolve the labor dispute and ensure the continued production of spruce (Ficken, 1987). Disque created two organizations, the Spruce Production Division and the Loyal Legion of Loggers and Lumbermen (known as the 4L). The latter organization, according to Ficken, "served as a rallying point for employers and workers opposed to the IWW. . . . With mill and camp employees required to join the 4L and known Wobblies barred . . . the Legion went a long way toward eradicating radical influence" (1987: 147). The eight-hour day was eventually accepted by the operators. As Ficken points out, observers and historians have disagreed over which side "won" the battle:

> To a great many observers, including subsequent historians, the strike resulted in a triumph for labor. Through the instrumentalities of military power and persuasive personality, Colonel Disque, went the argument, had forced a reluctant industry to adopt a great reform. Even

for hard-line lumbermen, however, the eight-hour day had never been of crucial importance. Essentially, the industry concluded the same arrangement first proposed in the summer of 1917:   the eight-hour day for a government crackdown on the Wobblies. Lumbermen traded something of modest significance for something of great consequence and emerged as the great victors in the strike (Ficken, 1987: 149).

The war itself also played a role in these events as the tide of public opinion turned against the IWW, whose leaders were defined as revolutionaries with communist sympathies detrimental to the war effort. A number of local towns in the region arrested or expelled IWW leaders during the period (Williamson, 1976). The Wobblies experienced a brief period of resurgence after the war, which included a general strike led by shipyard employees in Seattle in 1919 and the so-called "Centralia Massacre" of that same year. The latter event involved a battle between "Wobs" and American Legionnaires. The battle resulted in three Legionnaires' deaths and the subsequent lynching of Wobbly leader Wesley Everest. Seven Wobblies were eventually convicted of murder (Ficken, 1987). The Wobblies later suffered internal divisions, which increased their disfavor with the public, and their influence waned (Holbrook, 1938).

This era also saw the beginning of a new economic arrangement that profoundly affected logging in the region:

> The gyppo work pattern developed out of these changes adopted by the lumbermen. It began simply as a system of working by the piece, as an alternative to the newly established eight hour day. Piecework was seen as advantageous to both employer and employee. The logger working by the piece could work as long as he wished during the day because he was, in a sense an independent contractor. He was not on the company's payroll and he negotiated each job individually with the contractor or the company's woods boss (Williamson, 1976: 76).

The gyppo arrangement began to gain acceptance in 1917-1918 for tasks whose results were easily measured, such as timber falling, bucking and skidding. Other jobs, such as working on river drives or flumes, did not lend themselves to this arrangement, however. "Wage work" was to remain the dominant arrangement in Northwestern logging until the development of gasoline technology (Williamson, 1976).

Holbrook notes that the advent of the gyppo system was not received with universal acceptance in logging camps:

> In all camps, everywhere, bunkhouse forums discussed, and often blasted, the emerging gyppo, or contract system of woods work . . .

How it got its name nobody knows, but cynical old-timers said it came from gypsy, and especially the gypsy's well-known habit of taking everything not nailed down. You get the connection if you know what Wobblies term the "ideology of the class-conscious worker." That ideology is that the more you produce for the boss, the worse it is for you (Holbrook, 1938: 242).

As we will see in later chapters, whether or not Holbrook's interpretation of the origin of the term gyppo is correct, currently it is a point of pride among those to whom it is applied, rather than an object of derision.

In the post World War I period, life in the logging camps improved. Electricity was introduced. More civilized bunkhouses were built complete with windows, and spring cots with mattresses came into use. It was also during the post-war era that camp loggers acquired the "travel habit." While old-timers had been mostly content to stay in camp and "blow her in" only twice a year, this new breed of "short stakers" or "boomers" moved frequently from camp to camp, in some cases ranging from northern California to Alaska (Holbrook, 1938). Although little historical documentation exists concerning the specific migratory cycles of "boomers," there is evidence to suggest that there existed three geographically defined "circuits" in which they traveled, one centered around Seattle, one in southern Oregon and northern California, and one centered on Spokane (Schwantes, In press).

As the second world war approached, technological development continued to change the industry. Gasoline-driven equipment replaced steam and railroad logging. Trucks replaced railroad equipment for log hauling; bulldozers (cats) came into use for skidding logs; and portable "high lead" diesel and gasoline-driven yarders with towers replaced the steam donkey and spar tree arrangement. Diesel and gasoline-powered loaders replaced steam shovels for loading logs. In later years, rubber tired skidders were introduced, primarily because they create less soil disturbance than cats.

The gasoline-driven chain saw was surprisingly long in coming into acceptance. Charles Wolf developed a fairly workable model in the 1920s, but loggers initially rejected the technology (Lucia, 1975). Beginning in 1936, the H. A. Stihl Company of Germany exported a lightweight chain saw that did receive some use in Canada, but failed to generate much interest in the United States. Supplies of that saw were soon cut off by the war. Finally, the development of the Omark chain by Joe Cox, a Portland, Oregon, logger led to the acceptance of the chainsaw by Northwestern loggers. The new style chain soon proved itself in salvage logging in the Tillamook burn in Oregon, and the misery whip became quickly obsolete (Lucia, 1975). These technological changes were accompanied by changes in the way of life in the logging camps:

> That is, except in camps which are not camps at all, such as that of a large redwood operation where there are no camp buildings of any kind, everybody drives his car to and from his home in one of five towns within a radius of thirty miles of "camp" (Holbrook, 1938: 253).

In the early 1940s the sociologist Norman Hayner described the transition:

> The old-time (steam) logger, whether a "bull whacker" or a "donkey puncher" seldom married. . . Although the modern (petroleum) logger may have a keen interest in his forest work and be proud of the machine tools with which he is so skillful, he is much more likely to be married than the early day lumberjack and often returns every night to his home on a "stump ranch" or in a small town (Hayner, 1945: 218).

Hayner went on to described the gasoline logger as "domesticated" and "a family man" (1945).

Following the traumatic years of the Great Depression in which logging unemployment, like most other types in the country, hit an all-time high, the World War II period was one of severe labor shortages in the woods brought on by the need for able bodied workers for the military and the shipyards. By 1942 the labor shortage in the industry was described as a crisis, with workers finding themselves in a "seller's market" (Robbins 1988).

Robbins describes the post war era as the "[H]eyday of the storied gyppo logger and sawmill operator":

> Reckless and daring gamblers, always ready to move on to the next stand of timber, the multitudes of gyppos were unique to the postwar era in the Douglas-fir country. Opposed to labor unions and government regulations, they were a throwback to an earlier day of independent entrepreneurship. . . . Varying in size from three to fifteen or twenty employees, those small units were important contributors to the Coos economy between 1946 and 1960 (Robbins, 1988: 110).

In 1976 Williamson described the circumstances of the post war logger in a somewhat different tone:

> By 1950, the old-time lumber jack had virtually vanished, and the gyppo in particular had evolved from the contemptible pieceworker of the early 1920s to the independent, self employed, and respectable logger and family man that he is today. The nature of logging and the

organization of the work, has changed completely from the earlier, pre-World War II days of horses and hay, remote winter camps, river driving, and a winter work pattern, to a greater reliance on mechanized equipment, a predominantly summer work pattern, and the use of smaller crews performing the complete stump-to-mill process (Williamson, 1976: 81).

The 1970s saw continued advances in logging technology. Logging with hot air balloons was attempted and largely discarded as economically impractical (Roberge, 1991). Helicopter logging was tried and proved to be successful under certain circumstances. As always, technological change had social consequences. Describing the situation in Oregon, Robbins writes:

> Simply put, the mechanization of the forest products industry was diminishing the size of the work force. The changes in the south coast economy reflected a general transformation that has affected the North Pacific slope lumber industry, especially during the last twenty-five years. Dramatic technological and capital shifts--increased mechanization in the woods, the introduction of automated mill equipment, and centralized production in fewer plants--have altered both the productive base of the industry and the size of the work force. While large population centers with diversified economies like Portland, Seattle, and Vancouver, British Columbia, have been better able to withstand those dislocations, that has not been the case with smaller timber-oriented communities (Robbins, 1988: 153-154).

The macro-economic situation faced by the industry in a global economy has been, and continues to be, the subject of fairly intense scrutiny. What has not been as well studied or documented is the way of life of the workers in an era of uncertainty, created both by economic fluctuation and change and rapidly occurring political developments, relating to forest land use and regulation. It is toward a better understanding of the lifeways of woods workers and the impact of certain changes that the efforts of the studies reported here were directed.

Notes on Some More Contemporary History

The Evolution of Federal Timber Policy in the Pacific Northwest

The importation from Europe of professional forestry and its central technology, sustained yield timber management, to the U.S. was largely a result of public concern about the long-term consequences of unregulated timber harvest both for society at large and for timber-dependent communities (Clary, 1986). The central idea of sustained yield forestry is quite simply to allow only as much timber in a specified area to be harvested as can be replaced by regrowth in a given time period. Pinchot and his early successors in the Forest Service administered the national forests under a very loose statutory definition of sustained yield provided by the agency's Organic Act of 1897, which stated only that the lands were to provide a "continuous supply" of wood for the "use and necessities" of the nation (Behan, 1978; Clary, 1986). Sustained yield timber regulation was to become an issue at several points over the succeeding ninety years, more often than not, in reference to the Northwest (Lee, 1982).

The further specification of sustained yield did not receive much attention again until the 1930s when the timber industry was affected by difficult economic times. During that decade, a movement led by forester David T. Mason advocated the establishment of sustained yield units; some of which (labeled cooperative units) were to consist partly of national forest and partly of industry lands. This arrangement would grant the company in question effective monopoly control of the federal timber in the area in return for an obligation to practice sustained yield regulation on the combined lands. The objective was to stabilize both lumber prices and local communities, ironically in the face (in the short term, at least) of *over* supply. As we noted previously, Mason's vision was transformed into law with the passage of the Sustained Yield Forest Management Act of 1944. Although a number of units consisting of entirely federal land were created, only one cooperative sustained yield unit was ever established (a unit involving the Simpson Logging Company in Shelton, Washington). Other proposed cooperative units were opposed, both by labor and small timber operators (Clary, 1986)

As we suggested in the introduction, federal timber regulation did not become a serious national issue again until timber became a more sought-after commodity in the post World War II industrial boom, when clearcutting became an environmental issue (Dana and Fairfax, 1980) and thus a catalyst for further dissension. Although environmentalists brought the agency to court over clearcutting and other related silvicultural practices in the Bitterroot National Forest in Montana, they also charged the agency with "overcutting," that is to say, violating sustained yield. Stung by having their own doctrine used against them in court, the Forest Service administrators admitted to the existence of errors in inventory data that had resulted in overcutting on some national forests (Behan, 1978). In 1973, the agency issued Emergency Directive 16, which specified that all harvesting on national forests be regulated under the technical variant of sustained yield, known as "non-declining even flow" (Dana and Fairfax, 1980).

As the name implies, non-declining even flow (NDEF) is a two part concept. Even flow simply implies equal periodic yields of timber. The "non-declining" component refers specifically to old-growth "surplus forests". From the unitary standpoint of timber production, the maintenance of old-growth stands is considered inefficient, because such stands have reached biological maturity and produce relatively little additional volume. One school of thought in forestry advocates harvesting old-growth stands at faster than immediately sustainable rates to make way for young stands in order to achieve the appropriate age distribution of a normal forest more quickly. This strategy, it is argued, would increase the volume of wood produced in the long run by freeing up the land upon which old-growth is currently found to produce new wood. Non-declining even flow prevents this rapid liquidation by specifying that only the given *volume* (measured in board feet or cubic feet) of wood that can be replaced by regrowth in a specified time period (in this case ten years) may be harvested. Because old-growth trees are so large, the volume removed from a single acre typically equals the regrowth potential of many acres of second-growth trees for a given time period. Thus NDEF results in a slower "conversion" of old-growth to second-growth stands than other models previously applied. Consequently, it is considered a very conservative variant of sustained yield. Mainstream environmental groups supported the adoption and continuation of NDEF policies on national forest lands in the 1970s and early 1980s because it slowed "conversion", while the industry was generally very much opposed for the same reason (Dana and Fairfax, 1981).

Adams and Haines (1990) noted this and other developments in federal timber policy during that period:

> By the late 1960s, harvest was approaching maximum levels under current management plans and Forest Service timber policies began to change. Computation of allowable cut levels was shifted to a non-declining even-flow basis. Wilderness legislation and the expansion of undeveloped reserves removed large areas from the harvestable base. In unreserved areas, harvest practices were modified to reduce environmental and non-commodity use impacts (Adams and Haines, 1990: 65).

Beginning in the 1960s, a number of forest economists and other policy commentators undertook an increasingly harsh critique of sustained yield and later NDEF. Building on the work of Ernest Gould

(1960; 1964), they argued that sustained yield had been developed during European feudalism under conditions of relative static population levels, relative scarcity of land in relation to capital, and stable technologies. They contended that none of those conditions fit the capitalistic economy of the modern U.S., and they argued for a more market responsive approach to federal timber regulation (Waggener, 1969, 1978; Behan, 1978). Reflecting this view, a special presidential advisory panel on Timber and the Environment recommended in 1973 that liquidation of old-growth timber on federal forest land in the Northwest be accelerated to achieve greater efficiency of production (LeMaster, 1984).

In the ensuing years, as the current national forest planning process unfolded pursuant to the National Forest Management Act of 1976 (NFMA), the advisability of "departures" from NDEF became an issue in the forest plans for the old-growth forests of the Northwest (Behan, 1978). Provisions for departures were included in the NFMA regulations and arguments were made that, in some cases, departures would benefit communities. Adams and Haines state: "Accelerated harvests from old-growth stocks on national forests, so-called 'departures,' have been seen as a potential vehicle for spanning near-term gaps in private cut" (1990: 69). They go on to note, however, "With the prospective expansion of old-growth withdrawals from the timber base, departure or departure-like actions may be effectively impossible" (1990: 69).

Although a departure alternative was never selected for a national forest, the net result in the Douglas-fir region of the events described above, in conjunction with the upswing in the forest products market, was a steady increase in national forest harvests throughout the 1980s from the record lows at the beginning of the decade. The levels reached by 1989 approached, but did not reach, those of the high production period of the 1960s and early 1970s. Other public lands in the region experienced similar harvest patterns (Adams and Haines, 1990). The draft national forest plans (pre-owl restrictions) projected a decrease in annual sales for the 1990s to 2.9 billion board feet in the region as compared to the 3.4 million averaged from 1977 to 1988, due in large part to reductions in the land base available for harvest (Adams and Haines, 1990). It should be noted that these reductions in the land base included one to three thousand acre set asides known as Spotted Owl Habitat Areas (SOHAs) designated in the owl region forest plans. As we will note below, the designation of SOHAs in the forest plans was the result of concern growing in the late 1980s about the viability of the spotted owl (USDA Forest Service, 1992a).

The Spotted Owl/Old-Growth Forest Controversy

Prior to the 1970s, the existence of endangered plant or animal species on particular sites had little effect on public timber harvesting activities. Perhaps the most important early impact on forestry activities in the West resulting from concern with endangered species was the Environmental Protection Agency's prohibition in 1972 of the use of the insecticide DDT (Dana and Fairfax, 1981). That prohibition, executed under the authority of the Federal Insecticide, Fungicide, and Rodenticide Act, was linked to concern about the chemical's effect on populations of birds of prey, including the American bald eagle. The act required western foresters to seek alternative measures for treating Douglas-fir tussock moth, a destructive pest of Douglas-fir forests.

The relative inattention of federal forest managers to endangered species was destined to change as a long-term result of the passage of the Endangered Species Act (ESA) in 1973 and NFMA in 1976. Even after these acts were passed, however, protection of endangered species did not have much impact on forest management in the West for several years, until national attention to a particular "indicator species", the northern spotted owl, began to emerge.

The northern spotted owl is a creature of the Douglas-fir forests of western Washington, western Oregon and northern California. Although little was known about this bird prior to 1970, research by a wildlife biologist, Eric Forsman beginning in 1972 (notably a year before the passage of ESA) suggested that this secretive bird requires habitat consisting of stands of Douglas-fir trees with particular characteristics (Yaffee, 1994). These characteristics include multistoried canopies, large stem diameter, and high canopy closure. It was also surmised that the presence of cavities for nesting, rotting trees, and downed woody debris for prey habitat are important for the owl's viability (Gutierrez and Cary, 1984; Thomas et al., 1990). Thus wildlife biologists came to [the] "conclusion . . . that northern spotted owls are dependent upon old-growth conifer forests of the Pacific Northwest" (Gutierrez, 1985: 39).

> Forsman and his advisor, Howard Wright were convinced that their early research indicated that the owl was in trouble, and they began to lobby for changes in policy and on-the-ground management to protect the owl while additional research was carried out. As leader of The Oregon Cooperative Wildlife Unit, a division of the U.S. Fish and Wildlife Service, housed at [Oregon State University's] Department of Fisheries and Wildlife, Wright was in a position to work through official channels. In July, 1972, only five months after Forsman began his studies, Wright sent identical letters to his boss in Washington D.C. and regional officials in the Forest Service and the BLM [Bureau of Land

Management], informing them of the early results of Foreman's research (Yaffee, 1994: 15).

Yaffee goes on to note that although the official responses of the agencies contained expressions of concern about the owl, any impact of the information on actual management practices was "questionable" (1994).

The first governmental entity to deal seriously with the spotted owl/habitat question was the state level Oregon Endangered Species Task Force, which began its work in 1973 (Yaffee, 1994).[1] The Task Force, which included representatives from the Forest Service, BLM, and U.S. Fish and Wildlife Service (FWS), adopted a set of recommendations that included setting aside 300 acres of habitat for each known pair of spotted owls.

In August of 1973 the Forest Service and the BLM rejected the recommendations on several grounds, including the desire to avoid temporary restrictions that might evolve into permanent management practices without adequate justification. Another reason was the potential magnitude and complexity of managing on the basis of the "moving target", provided by discovery of individual locations of animals (Yaffee, 1994). In 1978 the Task Force issued a management plan based on considerably more data than had been available in 1973. The plan called for the maintenance of at least 400 pairs of owls to be located primarily on federal forest lands in Oregon. This plan was to be accomplished by the maintenance of 1200 contiguous acres of forest per owl pair and was to include a core area of 300 acres of old-growth with management areas to the home range for a minimum of three owl pairs. These recommendations (to which the agencies ultimately agreed--and which proved to be mild compared to future habitat protection measures) served to get the attention of the federal land agencies and to move the owl/habitat issue into more central focus in the federal arena (Yaffee, 1994).

In the meantime, concern on the part of this relatively small group of biologists about the viability of owl populations exposed to the effects of any continued disappearance of habitat, coincided with the turning of regional and, subsequently, national environmental groups to the question of the remaining stands of old-growth Douglas-fir, located primarily on federal land in western Washington, Oregon, and northern California. Given the fact that there is no legislative protection for particular types or conditions of ecosystems, the groups evolved two approaches for using the spotted owl's circumstances, approaches intended to thwart plans already in place for eventually converting the remaining unharvested old-growth forests to second-growth stands:

Timber interests argue and environmental interests openly acknowledge that the spotted owls are not the real issue but are only a "surrogate" for the larger question of old-growth preservation (Johnston and Krupin, 1991: 617).

The first approach was to use the provisions of existing legislation relating to federal land management (notably the National Environmental Policy Act (NEPA) and NFMA) to attempt to influence agency planning and decision-making pertaining to owl habitat. To that end, environmental groups appealed the Regional Guide released by the Forest Service in 1984. The Regional Guide is a key document that fulfills part of the requirements of the agency's planning process for each of its regions. The groups claimed the guide did not take adequate account of biological information generated in the previous four years concerning the habitat requirements of the owl. They requested a regional level Environmental Impact Statement(EIS) on owl management covering both national forest and BLM lands *and* a moratorium on old-growth harvest in the meantime. To the surprise of many observers, the agency chose to prepare a Supplemental Environmental Impact Statement (SEIS) on the spotted owl but, not surprisingly, refused to grant the harvest moratorium (Yaffee, 1994). The preparation of the document put considerable pressure on agency decision makers:

> . . . comments reflected a developing split within the [Forest Service] staff as to the role of the agency and the need to be sensitive to political variables. For the research biologists, and some of the applied biologists. . . the primary concern was protecting habitat to insure a viable population of owls. For some of the managers and the policy level biologists . . . long-term political sustainability of an agency decision was most important, subject, of course, to estimates of what the political response would be to any given decision. They argued that if the agency went too far to the preservation side, the political fallout might harm long-term owl protection efforts, and even worse, have a backlash effect on the Endangered Species Act. To critics of this view, the backlash argument was just a shield for continuing business as usual . . . (Yaffee, 1994: 94).

In the end the decision announced in 1988 (in the form of the Final SEIS), described by the national leadership of the agency as balanced and reasonable, pleased virtually no one outside the agency; consequently, lawsuits from environmental groups and industry resulted (Yaffee,1994).

The other approach adopted by the environmental groups to protect old-growth was to use the Endangered Species Act. From the environmentalist's perspective, perhaps the most effective way to protect as many acres as possible of the remaining old-growth fir forests from harvest, it would be to persuade or compel the Fish and Wildlife Service, to "list" the owl as "threatened" or "endangered" under the terms of the ESA (Johnston and Krupin, 1991). This action would lead to a requirement for the maintenance and restoration of "critical habitat" for the species in an attempt to ensure its long-term survivability (O'Laughlin, 1992). In 1986 and 1987 environmental groups filed two petitions with the FWS asking it to list the owl in Washington, Oregon, and northern California. In December of 1987, the agency announced its finding that listing was not warranted at that time (Thomas et al., 1990). A number of members of Congress became concerned about the FWS decision process, and a General Accounting Office (GAO) investigation was undertaken to examine that process (Johnston and Krupin, 1991). In addition, a lawsuit was filed in federal court the next year by the Sierra Club Legal Defense Fund to attempt to force the agency to review its decision (Thomas et al., 1990).

The court found in favor of the plaintiffs stating that the FWS decision was "arbitrary and capricious". The court also directed the agency to provide analysis to support its decision. The FWS formed a new review team to reexamine the matter. In February, 1989 the GAO released a report stating that "FWS staff had buckled to political pressure not to list the owl." In April, 1989 the FWS issued a "proposal to list" the owl as "threatened" throughout its range in the three states. The listing was finalized in June of 1990 and was quickly followed by lawsuits by environmentalists against both the Forest Service and the BLM, seeking injunctions to halt timber sales in owl habitat. (Johnston and Krupin, 1991: 621).

The myriad of events that unfolded during, and in the wake of, the Final SEIS and the listing decision and the resulting lawsuits and injunctions are too complex and involved to detail fully here; however, some of the more significant occurrences will be briefly noted. Among these were a series of "yellow ribbon" demonstrations by loggers and their sympathizers throughout the region beginning in early 1989 and extending into 1990:

> On February 28, 1989, more than 400 loggers staged a rally on the steps of the state capitol in Olympia, Washington, and then marched on a "friendly" Washington State Senate committee to demand passage of anti-set-aside legislation. . . More than 150 truck rigs clogged the area around the the capitol, horns blaring. State Senator Amondson hoisted his young son aloft and received 'a hero's welcome,' asking "is it spotted owls or kids? Our kids come first."(Yaffee, 1994: 114).

In June of 1989 there was an attempt at a negotiated settlement in a "summit meeting" of principles in the dispute, orchestrated by Senator Mark Hatfield, Representative Les AuCoin, and Governor Neil Goldschmidt, (all of Oregon). Three representatives of industry and three of environmental groups were included; the regional heads of the three federal agencies were also involved. Following structured discussions in the morning, Hatfield and AuCoin presented a proposed compromise, which included proposed specific harvest levels (roughly equivalent to those of recent years) from national forest and BLM lands for a two-year period. Also included in the proposed agreement was the understanding that all parties were required to drop injunctions on existing timber sales and were precluded from filing additional administrative appeals and injunctions on the timber sales programs in question for the same time period. In return, there would be language calling for non-fragmentation of significant stands of old-growth and explicitly stating that there would be no presuppositions about future land management decisions (Johnston and Krupin, 1991; Yaffee, 1994).

Johnston and Krupin (1991) reported the responses to the proposal:

> On Tuesday, June 27, 1989, citing too much uncertainty and too little time for careful consideration, environmentalists rejected the proposed timber compromise. Speaking for the Ancient Forest Alliance, Andy Kerr indicated that the conservationists were willing to continue negotiating. A temporary postponement in a key United States House of Representatives committee meeting provided the groups with another day for talks. Representatives of the timber industry expressed reluctant grudging support for the proposal.

> Larry Tuttle, the Oregon director of The Wilderness Society said that environmentalists probably would be willing to accept the harvest levels called for in the compromise. But Andy Kerr . . . indicated that environmentalists were unlikely to agree to such a sweeping withdrawal of federal court injunctions.

> On Wednesday, June 28, 1989, the proposed compromise appeared to fall apart when the environmentalists would not agree to the provisions of the plan. The environmentalists received much of the blame for the collapse of the plan (Johnston and Krupin, 1991: 632-633).

On Friday, June 14 the environmentalists released a counterproposal containing suggested harvest levels only slightly lower than those in the original proposal, but stating that such levels could not be maintained over time. The environmentalists' proposal called for a series of "screens" for accepting or rejecting timber sales designed to add considerable specificity to the nonfragmentation provisions. The environmental groups also proposed a narrower set of restrictions on appeals and injunctions (Yaffee, 1994).

The counterproposal was immediately rejected by the industry, the agencies and the Congressional delegation. The Forest Service took particular umbrage at the screens stating that they would constrain timber sales as badly as the injunctions in place at the time and make the achievement of stated harvest levels effectively impossible. (Yaffee, 1994). Congressional response to the failed settlement attempt was the passage of the so-called Hatfield-Adams Amendment (Section 318 of the Interior Appropriations Bill) in October of 1989, designed primarily to maintain federal timber harvest at previous levels in the "owl region" for another year:

> Section 318 established requirements for timber management practices on public forests for the period between October 1, 1989, and September 30, 1990. The act set forth substantive and procedural requirements and restrictions on the allowable levels to be cut, the fragmentation of remaining blocks of old-growth forest, the creation role and function of advisory committees, and limitations on judicial review (Johnston and Krupin, 1991: 636).

Among the substantive and procedural requirements were those requiring the Forest Service to provide the environmental groups a list of proposed timber sales from which the environmentalists could choose 1.1 billion board feet to be harvested, with the provision that the remaining sales on the list would not be offered during the end of the fiscal year. The bill also prohibited sales in known owl areas and provided for the creation of forest level citizen advisory boards to help the agency decide which areas would be harvested (Yaffee, 1994).

In April of 1990 the *Report of the Interagency Scientific Committee to Address the Conservation of the Spotted Owl* (Thomas et al., 1990) , hereafter known as the *ISC* or *Thomas* report (after its principle author, Forest Service research biologist Jack Ward Thomas) was released detailing a proposed conservation strategy for the spotted owl. The plan called for the creation by the year 2000 of large, habitat conservation areas (HCAs), some of which encompassed state and private land. Corridors of habitat would be maintained between these areas to ensure the owl's viability and genetic disbursement. The Chief of the Forest Service, Dale Robertson, stated that the implementation of the report's recommendations would result in harvest reductions of 1.0 to 1.3 billion board feet or 30 to 40 percent in the affected region. Industry analysts predicted job losses of 9,000 to 12,000 directly resulting from the plan's implementation (Yaffee, 1994).

In September, 1990, after considerable public controversy and media attention and an abortive attempt by the Bush administration to develop a plan independent of that of the ISC, the Forest Service announced its intention to manage the owl forests in a manner "not inconsistent" with the ISC report recommendations (USDA Forest Service, 1992). In the wake of the ISC report, Gorte (1992) drew the following conclusions concerning the probable impact of endangered species protection on federal timber harvest in the region:

> The amount of Federal timber sold in Washington, Oregon, and California in the future will undoubtedly be less than historic levels. As shown in nearly all the studies, the expected sales programs over the next decade under the final management plans for national forests in the area are expected to be lower than historic sales levels. Federal sales are expected to be about 4.2-4.4BBF [billion board feet] under the final plans after averaging 5.7 BBF from 1983-1987. The final plans probably include some spotted owl protection, but owl protection cannot be separated from other causes of the expected decline in timber sales under the final plans, and it is unclear whether owl protection is a major factor. The declines are significant and the impacts will be real, but cannot be attributed to spotted owl protection under the Endangered Species Act (ESA).
>
> Nonetheless, spotted owl protection under ESA will exacerbate the likely decline in future Federal timber sales. The ISC report is one widely accepted estimate of the protection needed on Federal lands to fulfill ESA . . . Under the ISC report, Federal timber sales are projected to decline by about 1.6 -2.0 BBF with much of the uncertainty in the decline in BLM sales . . . National Forest timber sales are projected to decline by about 1.3 BBF (40 percent) from the anticipated sale levels under the final plans. BLM sales are projected to decline by about 0.4 to 0.7 BBF (one- to two-thirds) under the ISC Report (Gorte, 1992: 10).

At the same time it announced its intention to follow the recommendations of the ISC, the Forest Service announced its intention to harvest 3.2 billion board feet of timber in the owl region for fiscal year 1991, an action that would entail harvesting in some roadless areas (areas not officially protected as wilderness but often treated as *de facto* wilderness) and in areas exempted from harvest the previous year by the advisory boards. In response, environmental groups sued the agency for proposing harvest without having a spotted owl management plan (complete with an Environmental Impact Statement, public notice, a Record of Decision etc.) in place (Yaffee, 1994). The result was first a temporary, and later a permanent, injunction against harvest until the agency produced a plan and EIS. These actions (the latter occurring in May, 1991) halted nearly 200 planned timber sales, effectively preempting logging on federal lands in the owl region (Scientific Analysis Team, 1993).

In February of 1991 the Fish and Wildlife Service named a Spotted Owl Recovery Team to designate critical habitat for the spotted owl as required by ESA and ordered by Federal District Judge Thomas Zilly (USDA Forest Service, 1992):

> The Fish and Wildlife Service initially proposed 11.6 million acres of critical habitat. After a public comment period, this total was reduced to 8.2 million acres . . . After further public comment, the Fish and Wildlife's final determination of critical habitat designated 6.9 million acres arranged to mimimize impacts on private lands (Scientific Analysis Team, 1993)[2].

During May of 1991, the Agriculture Committee and the Merchant Marine and Fisheries Committee of the U.S. House of Representatives created a panel of four scientists (titled officially as the Scientific Panel on Late-Successional Forest Ecosystems, but which became commonly known as the "Gang of Four") to develop and evaluate an array of alternatives for managing forests in the owl region. This panel and its report broadened the discussion of the forest issue to include all relevant vertebrate species, fish, and "ecosystem integrity". The report outlined fourteen alternatives, including risk assessments for species; it also contained projected timber harvest levels and estimated job impacts. (Scientific Analysis Team, 1993)

In June of 1992 the Fish and Wildlife Service announced a proposal to add the Marbled Murrelet, a small seagoing bird that inhabits the coastal areas of the Douglas-Fir region, to the federal list of threatened species (FEMAT, 1993).

In September of 1991, the director of the Bureau of Land Management invoked the 1978 amendments to the Endangered Species Act to request a hearing by the Endangered Species Committee (popularly known as the "God Squad") to consider exempting planned timber sales from owl-related restrictions on 4,426 acres of BLM lands in Oregon (O'Laughlin, 1992). The hearings, which received wide media coverage, featured testimony from timber families as well as habitat protection advocates. The result was as follows:

> In May, 1992, the God Squad decided to exempt 1,700 acres of timber sales in two heavily timber-dependent counties, and upheld protection on the remaining 2,726 acres. Owl protection advocates claim this is a

disaster, although 6.9 million acres have been designated as critical habitat. Timber processing advocates claim this is a disaster, too, saying all 4,226 acres should have been exempted (O'Laughlin, 1992: 11).

In response, the Portland Audobon Society sued the Endangered Species Committee, alleging that the committee had acted in violation of the Administrative Procedures Act by virtue of close consultation between the God Squad and the Bush White House and the lack of documentation of these contacts in the official record of the proceedings. In early 1993, the court found in favor of the plaintiffs and held that the record must be supplemented and the matter brought back to the court before the God Squad's decision could be implemented (Environmental Reporter, 1993). In the meantime, however, the White House had changed hands and the matter was apparently dropped.

In early 1992 the Forest Service released the *Final Environmental Impact Statement on Management for the Northern Spotted Owl in the National Forests* detailing its decisions concerning management of owl habitat. In the summer of that year, a federal judge remanded the matter back to the agency citing a lack of consideration of "recent scientific findings" concerning the owl as the problem with the report. In a separate action, he ordered the agency to come up with a revised plan. The agency was given a deadline of one year (Scientific Analysis Team, 1993).

In November, 1992 William J. Clinton was elected President of the United States. During the election campaign, he promised labor leaders in the Pacific Northwest and others that, if elected, he would hold a summit meeting to bring together a wide range of interests in an attempt to resolve the forest controversy (Forest Ecosystem Management Assessment Team or FEMAT, 1993). On April 2, 1993 the president made good on his promise and convened a one-day Forest Conference, which was televised throughout the nation. This extraordinary event included the Vice President, seven Cabinet members, a number of the region's political leaders, leading scholars and scientists and representation from across the spectrum of stakeholders in the controversy. Among those giving testimony were loggers and spouses of loggers.

At the end of the day, the president announced that he was directing responsible officials within the government to develop a plan to "break the gridlock" over federal forest management in the region. To that end, Clinton created three interagency working groups: the Forest Ecosystem Management Assessment Team, the Labor and Community Assessment Team, and the Agency Coordination Team. Further, he laid out five principles to guide their efforts:

First, we must never forget the human and economic dimensions of these problems. Where sound management policies can preserve the health of forest lands, sales should go forward. Where this requirement cannot be met, we need to do our best to offer new economic opportunities for year-round, high wage, high skill jobs.

Second, as we craft a plan, we need to protect the long-term health of our forests, our wildlife and our waterways. They are a . . . gift from God; and we hold them in trust for future generations.

Third, our efforts must be, insofar as we are wise enough to know it, scientifically sound, ecologically credible, and legally responsible.

Fourth, the plan should produce a predictable and sustainable level of timber sales and nontimber resources that will not degrade or destroy the environment.

Fifth, to achieve these goals, we will do our best, as I have said, to make the federal government work together and work for you. We may make mistakes, but we will try to end the gridlock within the federal government and we will insist on collaboration not confrontation (FEMAT, 1993: *ii*)).

As the name implies, the Agency Coordination team performed no analysis, but rather took on interagency coordination responsibilities. The primary result of the work of the Labor and Community Assessment team was the announcement of the Economic Adjustment Initiative, an effort to coordinate the efforts of 17 existing federal programs to assist workers and communities effected by reductions in federal timber harvest (Tuchmann, 1994). FEMAT created a series of ten options for managing the forests in question and performed assessments concerning the ecological (terrestrial and aquatic), economic, and social impacts of selected options. The options each divide the lands into categories for which particular management emphases and techniques are specified. The principle differences among options are the numbers of acres given over to each category and the details of how land in each category is to be managed. The categories include Congressionally Withdrawn Areas, Administratively Withdrawn Areas (constant across options) Late-Successional Reserves, (areas in which timber harvest is forbidden or severely limited) and Managed Late-Successional Reserves. The latter are areas in which a wider variety of silvicultural techniques are to be used, though an emphasis is placed on maintaining late successional (old-growth forests). The other categories include Riparian Reserves (areas managed primarily to protect riparian areas) and Matrix lands (areas in which a full range of silvicultural techniques are allowed).

In the summer of 1993, the administration announced its proposal to adopt as the President's Forest Plan, Option 9 of FEMAT. This option combines features of the "Gang of Four" Report, The Scientific Analysis Team Report, and the Forest Service's Draft Recovery Plan for the Northern Spotted Owl. The option called for annual harvests from the federal forests of 1.2 billion board feet of timber annually over the first decade. This represents approximately one fourth the average federal harvest levels of the 1980s; however, it is still only about one half of that which would have been allowed if ISC recommendations had been adopted in conjunction with the final Forest Plans. In late February of 1994, as it released the Final Environmental Impact Statement to accompany the President's Forest Plan, the administration revised the annual harvest estimates downward to 1.1 billion board feet to increase the size of some "buffer strips" along streams to increase protection for some fish species, notably salmon (Lewiston Morning Tribune, 2/24/94).

Option 9 also included provisions for ten Adaptive Management Areas in the owl region. These are landscape units ranging in size from 84,000 to approximately 400,000 acres. The FEMAT report states:

> The overarching objective for Adaptive Management Areas is to learn how to do ecosystem management in terms of both technical and social challenges . . . It is hoped that localized, idiosyncratic approaches that may achieve the conservation objectives of this plan can be pursued. These approaches rely on the experience and ingenuity of resource managers and communities rather than traditionally derived and tightly prescriptive approaches that are generally applied in the management of forests (III-24).

The report goes on to state that the propose locations for Adaptive Management Areas were selected to "minimize risk to the overall conservation strategy", but that proximity to communities subject to adverse economic impacts of reduced harvest of federal timber was also a consideration.

Meanwhile, in the post-FEMAT period, new contentions began to surface that the spotted owl may be more plentiful than had been assumed. One journalist who has followed the issue wrote:

> The owl extinction alarm is predicated on two notions: that spotted owl live only in ancient forests, and that a last fragile dwindling population of the northern spotted owl exists mainly in Oregon and Washington. New research suggests that neither notion is true. California does not end at the Golden Gate; between there and Oregon lies a 300 mile corridor of mostly Sierra Nevada forest. This vast

woodland, ignored in the owl debate, may contain a profusion of spotted owls (Easterbrook, 1994: 23).

The author goes on to note however, that environmentalists dispute these contentions suggesting that the owls have been driven to locations where they have been found in California as a result of old-growth logging in other locations. Further, environmentalists responding to the argument that spotted owls as a species may not be at the level of risk previously thought, respond that owls, under most circumstances, require very specialized habitat for long-term survival, namely the canopies of old-growth trees. Noting that the owl data Esterbrook cites were collected mostly in redwood stands, Koberstein (1994) states:

> The redwood data are troubling to some owl biologists, but not because they are invalid. It has been well known for a long time that a large number of owls live among young redwood stands. But the redwood owl data are the exception, not the rule, for a species whose range extends from San Francisco to the Canadian Border and beyond. Owls are thought to survive well in redwood stands because the trees there quickly regenerate.
> . . . North of the Oregon-California boarder, however, where slower growing Douglas firs dominate the landscape, no evidence shows the owl in good health (10).

The authors go on to cite the opinion of Oregon State University owl biologist Charles Meslow that the owl may be facing a "bottleneck" point beyond which it may not survive.

Clearly, the viability of the spotted owl and its relationship to particular forms of habitat remains controversial. Reflecting this controversy, and its relationship to the broader issue of the old-growth forests and the associated polarization over the latter issue, Easterbrook reports the results of an interview with Jack Ward Thomas, now Chief of the Forest Service:

> Thomas, whose owl gloom work won his national standing among environmentalists, was recently named by Clinton as the first biologist to head the Forest Service. Placing a biologist in charge of the agency is an excellent idea, since the protection of biodiversity should be a higher government priority than the felling of trees. But will the doomsday thinking serve the Forest Service any better than its previous adoration of the chainsaw? "It may well be that there are a significant number of northern spotted owls on private lands in California, but so what?" Thomas told me. "The injunction controls the issue now." (Easterbrook, 1994: 27)

Despite the continued dispute over the owl itself, by the post-FEMAT period it was clear that the environmentalists and their supporter-biologists in the federal land management agencies[3] had been successful in broadening public issues linked to the old-growth forests to encompass such diverse considerations as the marbled murrelet, the declining salmon runs in the region's river system, and questions of habitat fragmentation and forest land use throughout the owl region and beyond. Thus, when on June 6, 1994, in response to the FEMAT report and the President's forest plan, Judge Dwyer (at least temporarily) lifted the injunction, it was not clear that the action would have a particularly noticeable effect on timber harvesting in the owl region (Lewiston Tribune, 6/7/94).

Timber Supply, Jobs, and Impacts

Analysts of nearly all stripes agree that the halting or significant reduction of timber harvest on federal lands in the "owl region" is not of minor economic significance to the specific locations affected. Although the National Forests constitute only about forty percent of the region's available commercial forest land, they represent a much larger share of the stands old enough to harvest in the next two decades (USDA Forest Service, 1990; Adams and Haines, 1990).

Moving beyond this very general conclusion, however, to say that there has been considerable controversy, both in the technical literature and in the media, over the probable social and economic impacts of timber harvest reductions in the "owl region" is clearly an understatement. For example, in discussing job loss estimates, one set of authors notes:

> For many policy makers and concerned citizens, these reports have caused as much confusion as clarification. Projections of employment effects vary widely -- one projects a decline by [the year] 2000 of less than 12,000 jobs while another asserts that as many as 147,000 jobs will be lost (Sample and Le Master, 1992b: 31).

Even more striking is the discovery that some of the most respected names in the fields of forestry, policy analysis, and applied economics and sociology are associated with highly differing analyses of issues linked to the controversy. Two such issues have been of particular strategic importance to the politics driving the issue:

1. how to characterize the "pre-owl restriction" timber supply situation in the Douglas-fir region;

2. the relative impacts that technological advances in processing and other economic changes in the industry are having on wood products jobs versus those of supply restrictions.

These two issues are, in turn, linked to a broader question, namely:

3. the extent to which changes (and the magnitude of changes) faced by workers and communities as a result of the owl/forest question were or were not inevitable, and whether or not such changes are merely being accelerated by the controversy and its outcome.

The first two issues will be briefly discussed here, while the third issue will be revisited below.

At first glance, it might appear that commentators and analysts concerned with these issues are merely being selective, whether knowingly or not, in their use of specific "facts" to substantiate a particular analysis or conclusion. There are differences among analyses; for example in "before " and "after" time periods chosen, as well as whether the comparisons are harvest volumes or employment effects. Some analyses consider only "direct" timber jobs, while others look at "indirect" and "induced" jobs linked to timber processing. There are also discrepancies between "employment multipliers" used to estimate jobs of various types created or maintained per unit of timber processed. Still further differences exist in assumptions about the specifics of the land base which provides the basis of the various calculations (Gorte, 1992; Sample and Le Master, 1992a, 1992b).

Careful examination suggests, however, that there are more fundamental issues driving differences behind the impact analyses, in particular, how their results are interpreted, than the differences in studies noted above. In a recent book on technological decision-making and political choice, Schwartz and Thompson (1990) take issue with the clear distinction that many authors make between "facts" and "values" when going about impact analyses.

Those who study and analyze technological decision disputes have failed to recognize that any demarcation between factual impacts and social value dimensions in technological choice is, in itself . . . controversial. . . . They have failed to acknowledge that processes of impact 'assessment' are inherently ambiguous and , as such, are always open to political debate. What is considered a technical fact, and what is seen as belonging to the realm of social values, needs to be treated as part of the . . . dispute. . . . What is lacking in most of the literature is the acknowledgment that impact assessments, far from reflecting conflicting evaluations of the facts, involve rival *interpretive frames* in which facts and values are all bound up together. (Schwarz and Thompson, 1990: 22-23)

Questions involving timber supply and job impacts related to the owl/forest controversy are clearly bound up in competing interpretive "frames". It will be helpful to briefly explore how this has played out in the case of timber supply assumptions in the Douglas-fir region. As we noted above, most foresters, and probably most politicians, long assumed that the old-growth Douglas-fir forests on public lands in western Washington, Oregon, and Northern California would be eventually cut over and replaced by second-growth stands. The only real argument for years in forest policy circles was how gradually or precipitously this "stand conversion" would take place. Nearly everyone also recognized that the forest industry in the region had, in the post-war period, cut more timber on its own lands than could be replaced in the short term. This would require the industry to increase its dependence on federal timber in the 1990 to 2020 period.

The latter point led to two related disagreements. One disagreement concerned whether or not there would be sufficient federal timber to meet the demand during this thirty year period. As Le Master and Sample (1992) point out, a number of reports were written beginning in 1963, predicting a timber shortfall in the Douglas-fir region during the 1990 to 2020 period. On the other hand, others in the profession disagreed with the reports, saying that they were part of the discredited "forestry mythology" of the coming "timber famine".

The two most dramatic facts in a long history of forest utilization have been the near fourfold increase in wood growth in the past 60 years and the persistent and major underestimate by the U.S. Forest Service of the wood production potential of American Forests (Clawson, 1979: 1168).

Timber depletion has been an off-and-on issue in the world at least since the time of Solomon and the Cedars of Lebanon, and in North America since 1546 when the Viceroy of Mexico called attention to short fuelwood reserves. In the United States, it was a justification for the creation of the Forest Service and has been a continued theme in projections of the Forest Service, presidential commissions, and private researchers. The Douglas-fir region has been the specific subject of several of these reports.

In spite of these fears, we have never run out of timber, and contemporary analysts know that it is unlikely we ever will (Hyde, 1980: 135-136).

The critics of the timber shortage contention argued that:

1. capital investment in intensive forest management is the real limiting factor in wood production,
2. any potential timber short fall would be made up for by more intensive management on highly productive private and public lands as well as by entry into the market by small private non-industrial forest land owners.

Both these events, it was suggested, would be triggered by market signals.

The other disagreement, related to the increased dependence on federal timber, concerns whether the industry and its workers have a "right" to expect that timber would continue to be produced from federal lands at anything approximating previously planned levels. As we have noted, environmental legislation and other events that preceded the spotted owl controversy by more than twenty-five years (albeit in fits and starts related to the politics of the moment) steadily reduced the base of federal lands from which timber could be produced. The trend in legislation was clear.

From the interpretive frame of most environmentalists, these changes were long overdue and necessary to protect valued components of the forest ecosystem. From the point of view of most of the industry and many in the forestry profession, they were an endless ratcheting down of the availability of a renewable resource. When the crunch came in the form of the owl/old-growth issue, each side blamed the other for being short sighted on matters of timber supply. In drawing such a conclusion, the environmentalists' arguments generally factored in the growing harvest restrictions as a given and treated demand for particular harvest levels as a variable, while the industry generally took exactly the opposite view, seeing economic demand as a given and restrictions as a variable. Each then blamed the other for the crunch.

In light of the above discussion, what is fair to say about the timber supply situation in the owl region?

1. The disagreements and confusion concerning timber supply arise as a result of a complex set of interactions. For example, one person's source of timber is another's (intact or not-so-intact) forest habitat (Greber and Johnson, 1991). Another complication is not knowing for sure how dramatically non-federal (especially small, private, non-industrial) forest landowners in this and other regions (and indeed, other countries) will react to higher timber prices.

2. In addition to the complexity created by the interaction of a number of converging factors related to timber supply, each is complicated in its own right. It is probable, for example, that there would be more trees to harvest now if forest industry had been more conservative in cutting on its own lands, whatever the tradeoffs in terms of wood availability and housing prices during the post-war housing boom. Similarly, there would be more harvestable volume available if more investment in intensive forest management had been made sooner on highly productive managed sites across all forest ownerships in the region.[4] It is also quite probable that there would be more trees to cut now if forest managers in the public and private sector had been more responsive to shifting public perceptions and values about management practices, and, in particular, clearcutting. Obviously, there would be more trees to cut now if the decision had been made to continue converting the existing old-growth to managed stands. This, of course, was done, however haphazardly and with whatever costs in terms of habitat fragmentation and loss, in virtually all other forested regions of the country. The options in terms of old-growth management would also be different today if a conservation strategy for such forests had been developed 15 years ago, when the landscape was less fragmented than it is today. If such planning had occurred, there would have been at least the opportunity for more orderly shifts in harvesting patterns in the public and private sector.

3. Time is a critical variable in understanding the timber supply situation. The entire controversy can be framed as a planning horizon problem, as illustrated by the last point above, and by the realization that increased harvests from industry lands is highly probable, beginning in about twenty years as second-growth on industry lands matures.

As in the case with timber supply, differing frames of analysis have been adopted concerning estimates of employment impacts due to habitat protection on federal forests. In an analysis carried out after the ISC report, but before the Forest Conference and FEMAT, Sample and Le Master (1992A, 1992B) analyzed the approaches, assumptions, and results of several economic impact studies concerned with owl habitat protection. They noted:

In both the TWS [Wilderness Society] and AFRA [American Forest Resources Alliance-an industry group] studies, technological change and reduced forest-plan harvest levels account for about two-thirds of the timber industry decline expected by 2000 when the ISC strategy is applied on federal lands . . . This brings the net estimated employment decline to 11,858 and 32,015 jobs respectively. (Sample and LeMaster, 1992b: 33-34)

Unfortunately, as of this writing, the above mentioned studies have not been updated and republished to reflect the much more dramatic harvest reductions called for in Option 9. The only job displacement estimates currently available that refer specifically to the President's Forest Plan are in the FEMAT document itself and updated estimates which appeared in the Final Environmental Impact Statement (FEIS) for the President's Forest Plan published in the spring of 1994. The basis of comparison used in FEMAT is derived from 1990 employment levels with the range of displacement estimated to be from 21,200 to 32,000 jobs (1,700 to 12,500 in comparison to 1992). The report notes that these adjustments do not factor in technological change, but states that technological change may lead to an *increase* in jobs per unit of output ". . . when the focus is on raw material savings and product-improving technological change" (FEMAT: VI-29). The FEIS states:

In summary, these projections imply a range of job displacement arising from the proposed action from 4,600 to 15,900 jobs, relative to 1992. Compared to 1990, the potential displacement is 24,100 to 35,400 jobs. The relative differences to the time period of 1985 to 1989 have been added in thid Final SEIS and are 16,400 to 27,700 jobs. The Final SEIS job displacement estimates are higher than the estimates displayed in the Draft SEIS. The differences result from corrections in predicting nonfederal harvest levels and for Alternative 9, the reductions in [harvest levels] from federal forests resulting from changes in standards and guidelines, and land allocations between the Draft and Final SEIS. The majority of the affected jobs are in Oregon and are concentrated in southwestern Oregon (USDA Forest Service, 1994: 3&4-295).

The larger point remains that the specific numerical estimates are less important, both politically and conceptually, than understanding the framework in which they are presented and interpreted. One frame of reference suggests that the employment impacts involved in habitat protection are part of a larger (and implicitly inevitable) set of transformations occurring in forest communities. A competing frame of reference suggests that while some social and economic change is more or less "inevitable", the level and rapidity of impacts such as those occurring as a result of the owl/forest issue, remain, to a significant extent, a matter of social and political choice. Further, this perspective suggests that merely because the communities and workers are adjusting to the impacts from one source, such as technological change, is no reason to ignore or trivialize the impacts of another. Consider, for example, the following two quotations. The first is from the conclusion to the Sample and Le Master impact analysis comparison discussed above:

> The need to maintain old-growth forest habitat will magnify these effects in the near term because it collapses the time available to local communities to make the necessary adjustments. However, the change is fundamentally driven by factors other than habitat protection. This issue did not precipitate the situation, and allowing species dependent on old-growth to go extinct will not resolve it. Any viable long-term solution must take a comprehensive approach to the economic transition that is taking place in the Pacific Northwest and lay the foundation for ecologically sound regional prosperity and sustainable economic development in the future (Sample and Le Master, 1992b: 35).

Easterbrook (1994) casts the issue in a very different light:

> The lost jobs are high-wage employment of the sort that Americans who aren't lawyers or consultants need to send their children to college.
>
> If it is eventually understood that affluent environmentalists with white collar sinecure destroyed thousands of desirable skilled-labor jobs in order to satisfy an ideology and boost the returns on fund-raising drives, a long-lasting political backlash against environmentalism will set in. There is still time to avoid this turn of events. Ancient forests can be protected, additional timber jobs restored and the constructive political power of environmentalism sustained (Easterbrook, 1994: 29).

These conclusions differ in ways both obvious and subtle. Perhaps the most important difference is in the policy response that logically flows from each. If one adopts the Sample and LeMaster perspective, efforts to support local communities in these turbulent times merely delay an inevitable transition to a new sustainable future. Easterbrook might regard such a response as cavalier, perhaps dangerously so.

Attention will return in Chapter 6 to the impact of the spotted owl controversy and associated events on loggers and their families in study communities affected by the issue.[5] The intervening chapters will attempt to paint a picture of the loggers' way of life as observed and experienced in field studies by the author prior to the emergence of the owl/forest issue.

Notes

1. The description of policy related events in the owl/forest controversy, particularly those in the early stages, draws heavily on Yaffee (1994). For a more detailed discussion of such events (and a somewhat different interpretation of their meaning) the reader is directed to his book.

2. As Yaffe (1994) notes, public reaction to the critical habitat designation (particularly on private property) was strong. In anticipation of this, the notice that the agency produced in the action made it clear that private lands would only be affected if a federal permit were required. He also notes that the agency failed to carry out economic impact analysis as required by ESA and that the Secretary of the Interior has broad discretion to exclude areas from such designation so long as such an action will not result in the extinction of a species.

3. This is a coalition Lee (1993) labels an "epistemic community." However, from a sociological perspective, one can argue with this use of the term community (see Chapter Two). A more accurate phrase would be "epistemic coalition" to reflect the inherently instrumental/political nature of this set of relationships.

4. Many economists would argue that both harvesting rates and management intensity are in large part a function of economic incentives that are themselves affected by predictability of political processes. No particular disagreement with this perspective is implied here; rather, this point serves to further substantiate the contention that questions of timber supply are complex.

5. Before closing this chapter it should be briefly noted that the spotted owl/forest issue also has significance for revenues available for local and county level services, such as social services, roads, and schools. "Many rural counties and communities derive the majority of their revenue from timber harvest receipts and timber industry taxes. Counties receive twenty-five percent of the gross revenue derived from the sale of timber on [national forest] land. Oregon and California counties receive fifty percent of the timber receipts from BLM Oregon and California Act lands.

By agreement, timber revenue receipts from the [Forest Service] must be spent on public works and schools. In Oregon, seventy-five percent goes to public works. . . . The amount of money distributed in the form of revenues from the BLM and the [Forest Service] to counties in the Northwest from 1978 to 1988 is considerable. In 1988 alone, for example, revenue receipts were nearly $300,000,000 (Johnston and Krupin, 1992: 618-619)."

In a report completed in 1991, Lee et. al. examined probable impacts of declines in federal timber harvest revenues on county and local services in 11 timber producing counties in western Oregon dependent in part on the BLM Oregon and California Act lands mentioned above. The researchers developed scenarios of ten and fifty percent reductions in revenues, and interviewed a variety of county and local officials and service providers concerning probable impacts. The results generally indicated that "non-mandated" programs (i.e., libraries, parks, etc.) would bear the brunt of ten percent cuts while fifty percent cuts would be felt in "partially mandated" and non-mandated services as well (i.e., police and juvenile services, and so on). County and local service providers, particularly those in health care, expressed serious concerns about probable declines in program funding at a time when the need for services was likely to dramatically increase due to rising unemployment (Lee et. al.1991).

In a 1993 report focusing on BLM lands in western Oregon, Richardson notes: "Federal payments to counties have not yet declined to reflect the decline in federal timber receipts since 1990, due to Congressional "safety net" laws that have assured counties continued federal payments at close to their average annual payments in the late 1980s. . . Such compensatory payments are likely to be continued in some form under the FEMAT plan: the amount and duration of payments will be significant determinants of short-term impacts on county budgets and services, as will any other state or federal relief monies that may be directed to counties or local service providers (Richardson, 1993: 39)."

On the following page, however, the same author notes: "By the time of the July and August interviews, many counties had experienced some declines in federal timber revenues that county commissioners and other interviewees reported to be causing some county governments to cut back services and employment. (The federal "safety net" payments, while important, were still less than counties had received from federal timber revenues in the late 1980s.) Some people also noted that in addition to increased for services resulting from unemployment, local service demands were also increasing or expected to to increase due to inmigration of the elderly and of migrant workers, many of whom would need bilingual services (1993:40)."

4

Overview of the Northwestern Logger's Social World

The investigator's first task in the fieldwork for this study was to attempt to delineate the boundaries of the logger's social world. Following in the tradition of interpretive Sociology (see note at end of chapter), it would have been inappropriate to assume knowledge in advance concerning the attributes an individual needed to display to be considered a logger. The first order of business, therefore, was to attempt to discover empirically who is considered a logger and who is not. It was soon discovered that the boundaries are, in most cases, defined on the basis of technology and job function. Hence, much of the discussion herein is devoted to descriptions of the technology of logging. Considerable attention is also given to the responsibilities of, and interrelationships between, the incumbents in the various job roles.

It became obvious during the first days of the initial fieldwork that logging remains, at least in the study areas chosen for this research, very much a man's world. Of the individuals who were interviewed, and the several hundred who were encountered or whose names were located during the course of the studies, no women loggers were located. The author was given second- and third-hand reports concerning women loggers, but despite diligent efforts, was unable to locate a single female logger in the study area to interview. The major criterion for a man[1] to be defined as a logger is that he be (or have been, in the case of retired loggers) somehow involved in the process of moving logs from the stump to the mill. Anyone is included who builds logging roads or drives log trucks, as well as anyone involved in cutting and moving the logs from the stump to the landing.[2] Individuals whose primary responsibility is cutting and piling brush and logging debris are not ordinarily considered to be full-fledged loggers. Workers who plant trees after logging is completed, and those who scale (measure) logs at the mill are not logger group members.

Upon first discovery, these membership criteria seem arbitrary, but further investigation of the logger's value system revealed their logic. As was noted in the previous chapter, logging has historically been an extraction activity. Although the era of "cut out and get out" logging is over, some of the values developed in that period remain in the occupation. One of the ideas to survive is that "real logging" involves getting the wood to the mill. Brush cutting and reforestation are not part of the extraction process. This is not to say that the importance of reforestation is not appreciated or understood, but reforestation is seen as an activity that stands outside of logging.

The bond that links a group of highly individualistic and independent workers is the commitment to the task of "getting the logs to town". Loggers who are seen by their peers to lack this commitment rarely last in a job. If a crew member displays his lack of commitment by failing to "pull his weight", he is usually "sent down the road" in short order. If he is protected by a union or by some special relationship to a supervisor or owner, he is usually ostracized by his fellows. One logging boss for a large unionized company stated that he rarely had to start proceedings to fire a man who was not doing his job because the crew "would make the laggard's life so miserable" that he would usually leave of his own accord. In this sense loggers resemble the Salmon fishermen described by Miller and Johnson:

> [F]ishermen in the Bristol Bay are united by their reverence for the fishery as a whole. The occupational identity of commercial fishermen which all share, is made even more prestigious by the Bristol Bay connection. The uniqueness of the fishery in the eyes of the entire industry lends a special significance to being involved. Thus, simply being there . . . creates feelings of brotherhood (Miller and Johnson, 1981: 137).

However, Miller and Johnson also note that the fishermen's occupational community is far from being a seamless web and that social boundaries exist between subgroups. For example, ethnic subgroups tend to differentiate themselves from one another, as do full-time fishermen from "part-timers". The authors report evidence of stereotyping of one group by another.

The existence of boundaries, which are in some ways analogous to those reported by Miller and Johnson, was found in the case of loggers. Despite the bonds and symbols that link all types of loggers, there are important categories or subgroups. Perhaps the best analogy to use in describing these boundaries is to say that they are semi-permeable. Individuals do occasionally move from one subgroup to another, but there is a tendency for the worker to stay within one subgroup once having become established there. The reasons for this will be discussed below. A further point to be made concerning the subgroups is that they can be seen to be located on a continuum that ranges from those central in the loggers' work world to those on the periphery. To describe the situation in Orwellian language, some loggers are more "logger" than others. As will be discussed below, the location of the categories along the continuum is expressed in a number of subtle and not-so-subtle ways. The location of an individual within a particular category affects not only how others perceive him, but also how he perceives and defines himself.

The Organization of the Work and Its Implications

Gyppo Versus Company Logger

The term "gyppo" has remained a important term in the logger's world, although the fieldwork uncovered no evidence that the term is used perjoratively as Holbrook (1954) states it was in the first world war era. In fact, the prevailing view among those interviewed in these studies is that the origin of the term relates to the need for independent operators to move around like "gypsies", rather than any sense that the gyppo arrangement cheats anyone. In current times, gyppo logging "outfits" are relatively small, independently run operations with no land base of their own. The term is used most commonly to distinguish employees and owners of these smaller operations from those of larger, land holding companies.

Early in the fieldwork it appeared that this distinction constituted the only meaning of the word "gyppo". As the work progressed, however, the term was encountered in a variety of somewhat confusing contexts, and it became clear that it has additional related meanings. One such context was a gyppo logging operation in which the operator owned several trucks in addition to his logging equipment. If one applied the rule stated above, all of his employees including drivers would be called gyppos by virtue of the fact they worked for his independent operation. In this particular case, the operator contracted for the services of several individuals, each of whom owned and operated his own truck. These owner-operators who were paid on the basis of volume hauled per unit distance were referred to as the gyppo drivers, while those who were employed directly by the contractor were called "his" drivers. In this context, it is clear that the term "gyppo" is used in a relative sense to refer to those individuals who operate in the most independent mode.

Another related meaning for the term gyppo surfaced early in the study during an interview with a driver who owned and operated a single logging truck. He stated that he had considered himself a gyppo even during an earlier period when he drove for a larger company. When asked to explain this apparent contradiction, he stated that he had always been a gyppo in the sense that he drove extra fast and always "went after one more load" when given the chance. In short, he acted as if he was motivated by ownership of the truck even though he had been in fact working for wages. Thus this individual had taken on the identity "gyppo" well in advance of his being a gyppo in any "objective" economic sense.

As the fieldwork progressed, it became clear that the identity gyppo is used as a badge of honor. A gyppo woods logger, road builder, or truck driver places great value on his independence and freedom from the rules that constrain workers in larger organizations. Gyppos typically maintain that the small operations with which they are associated are inherently more efficient than larger organizations. This efficiency is attributed in part to the fact that the owner of the operation is frequently out on the ground working beside the crew or driving a truck alongside the other drivers. Gyppos hold a strong belief that supervision by individuals who are not experienced in doing the work themselves inevitably leads to inefficiency. "Dirty" logging bosses (that is, those who get dirty because they are actually doing part of the work) almost always command more respect than those who remain clean.

Gyppos see themselves as the direct heirs of the old-time loggers who settled the West and conquered the big timber through rugged endurance. They sometimes express disdain for company loggers who, in their view, "hide behind the union" to protect their jobs and who (again in their view) "are more interested in abiding by union regulations than getting the logs out." Gyppo rigging crews typically work ten or twelve hour days in the summer months while company crews work "only" eight or nine. Gyppos often view company crews to be over-staffed and under-productive. One gyppo logger who had worked for a large company for a number of years described a particular former company co-worker as someone whose friendship he values, but whom he would never hire because the co-worker is . . . "been in the union way of doing things for too long." He went on to state that the union "ruins" many potentially good young workers by discouraging them from producing at the highest possible level and from carrying out tasks outside of their job descriptions: "A good logger (who, for example, runs a piece of equipment) doesn't say no to setting chokers or bumping knots."

Company loggers also tend to be more security conscious than gyppos. An individual who joins a unionized company sees the years spent as an investment both in terms of promotions that result from seniority and the accrual of health and retirement benefits that gyppos rarely, if ever, have. When interviewed, company loggers often admitted that gyppo crews are more productive, but many questioned the costs of that productivity in terms of the hours an individual is required to work, as well as the strain that the gyppo pace places on the worker. Many company loggers consider gyppo logging to be young men's work. The immediate financial return to the gyppo employee is usually greater due to generally slightly higher wages and overtime pay. Company loggers emphasize that as a man gets older and his family's immediate cash needs decrease, that long-term health and retirement benefits become more important, and thus, in the long run, an individual is better off working for a company.

Despite their differences from gyppos, the company loggers interviewed and observed shared with them great respect for private enterprise in general and the entrepreneur in particular. Along with this attitude exists a remarkable lack of any vestige of union militancy or anti-company sentiment, even during times when workers are being laid off. The company is seen as a provider of jobs that otherwise would not exist. The union, typically viewed in the study area as a creature of mill employees rather than loggers, is looked upon with ambivalence. It is seen as a positive force insofar as it negotiates higher wages and additional benefits for woods workers. On the other hand, there is a common perception among the company loggers interviewed that union leadership's wage demands had been excessive, and thus had contributed to instability and unemployment in the industry. Many company loggers resent the union-backed seniority system and complain that the seniority rules often prevent the best workers from moving up to positions of responsibility and that less worthy employees gain promotions.

As was true in Hayner's era, even unionized company loggers often take great pains to disassociate themselves from millworkers. They often stereotype millworkers as "cry babies" who are unmotivated and unwilling to do "a day's work for a day's pay". One company logger proudly related an incident in which he and two others were the only woods workers to attend an important union meeting. According to his account, a resolution strongly supported by the millworkers, but requiring unanimous consent, was brought to the floor. The loggers voted against the resolution effectively killing it, but then felt compelled to leave the meeting hall quickly, as they feared for their safety.

In addition to the company gyppo dichotomy, there are other important subgroup boundaries within the logger's world. The four major categories -- timber fallers, rigging crew members, road building crew members, and log truck drivers -- all relate to job functions.

Fallers

Taken as a group, timber fallers, or bushelers as they are sometimes called, represent the elite of the working loggers. As was true in the early times, the faller's job is to cut the trees designated for harvest. Fallers are also charged with trimming off branches (limbing) and bucking the felled trees into usable log lengths. "Falling" standing trees is considered to be the most dangerous and highly skilled job in the woods. Individuals wishing to become fallers usually work several years bucking and limbing "behind" an experienced faller before they are allowed to work independently. Fallers are ordinarily paid on the basis of the volume of wood cut (measured in thousands of board feet) for a given "half" (half month pay period). In the case of gyppo operations, fallers subcontract with the logging contractor to fall, buck and limb the timber for a specified price per thousand board feet. The faller is responsible for furnishing his own pickup truck, saws, gasoline, oil and other related equipment. As an independent contractor, he is responsible for his own workman's compensation insurance and bears the risk of equipment breakdown. Fallers typically work in pairs, largely for safety reasons. In some instances, one faller acts as the contractor with the other as his employee, but most prefer to form a partnership. Some falling pairs "single jack", meaning that they fall, limb, and buck each tree. Others hire buckers. Buckers are usually paid a predetermined percentage of the fallers' rate applied to the amount of their individual production. Under usual conditions, a faller who does no single jacking requires two buckers to keep pace with him.

Company fallers are usually company employees and union members in a technical sense, but most company fallers in the study area are paid on a volume basis. In some cases, they furnish their own equipment; in others, it is supplied by the firm with a proportionate reduction in the rate of pay per thousand board feet produced. The faller's pay arrangement is a source of great pride because it reinforces their sense of independence. Even company fallers like to state that they really answer to no one but themselves because they are paid only for what they accomplish. Several fallers interviewed stated that they chafed when they were temporarily placed in the position of working for "day wages".

Although they are the highest paid laborers in logging, fallers ordinarily work the shortest hours. It is widely accepted that falling or bucking for more than six hours per day greatly increases the likelihood of accidents. Falling in particular requires close attention to detail and high level of alertness. Carelessness brought on by fatigue can cause an injury or a fatality. Several fallers related incidents in which a "sixth sense" had caused them to look up just in time to avoid being killed by a falling branch or chunk of rotten bark. Fallers take pride in their high status. One old-time faller stated that logging bosses tell the rigging crew what to do while directions to fallers are put in the form of requests. He stated that, in many instances, fallers can get away with refusing to carry out a request for a logging boss while a rigging crewman would be fired on the spot for a similar offense.

Fallers often begin their careers in the ranks of a rigging crew, but once having established themselves in falling, few ever return. This is partly due to the higher pay rates and shorter hours. It is also related, however, to their perceived independence. Nearly every faller interviewed listed a number of hardships associated with the job, including inevitable injuries, the high cost of equipment, and the necessity of often living away from home to work. Each of them stated that the main reason for staying in the job is the independence and the lack of necessity for cooperating with others that it affords. Even falling partners rarely work within fifty yards of each other. Each tree to be cut represents a challenge, and fallers derive satisfaction from facing that challenge alone.

The boundary between fallers and other loggers is reinforced by the fact that they spend so little time in contact with the crew. While a rigging crew typically commutes together to and from the job in owner-furnished vehicles and works more or less as a unit all day, fallers usually keep different hours and commute on their own. Interactions between fallers and rigging crewmen are infrequent and typically brief, because fallers nearly always work ahead of the crew. In some cases, supervisors ask fallers to make their early afternoon departures from the job as inconspicuous as possible to avoid resentment from the rest of the crew who all have several more hours to work.

The Rigging Crew

The group of workers charged with moving logs from where they have been falled and bucked to the landing where they are loaded onto trucks is called the rigging crew. There are three systems commonly used in the western United States for moving logs from the stump to the landing, but each requires the use of steel cables or rigging and hence the term.

Cat Sides

In logging parlance, the term "side" refers to the complete crew of workers and the associated equipment necessary to move logs from the stump to the truck. A side that uses bulldozers (cats) and rubber tired skidding tractors (skidders) to move (skid) logs is called a cat side. The rigging crew on a typical cat side consists of one or more cat or skidder operators (cat skinners), one choker setter per cat skinner, one or two landing chasers (knot bumpers) and a loader operator. Additionally, there is usually a foreman (ramrod or, more commonly, siderod). In the case of gyppo operations, the siderod is often a working foreman who, in addition to his managerial duties, performs one of the duties noted above.

Choker setters constitute the bottom of the status hierarchy on a cat side. The choker setter's job is to set (fasten) chokers (devices constructed from five- to eight-foot lengths of three-eighths inch diameter steel cable with a sliding bell attached) around logs so the logs can be moved by the cat or skidder. The cat or skidder is equipped with a winch and length of one- to one and one-half inch diameter steel cable known as the bowline. In many instances, the choker setter is required to manually pull a hundred or more feet of bowline from the winch to reach the logs to be skidded. Up to seven or eight logs can be taken to the landing per trip or "turn" as it is called. While the cat is returning to the landing with a turn of logs, the choker setter is expected to locate the next logs to be skidded and then to direct the cat to them upon its return.

Despite his relatively low status, the choker setter is a major determinant of the pace of the side. One worker on a logging job called choker setting the "fastest job in the woods". If the choker setter is slow in locating logs or in setting chokers, log production is reduced. Thus in both gyppo and company operations, new choker setters are given a few days or a week to prove they can handle the pace and stay out of danger. Those who cannot keep up are quickly fired. It is not unusual for a choker setter to be dismissed in the middle of the day and told to find a ride back to town on a logging truck.

Although some have prior connections to logging through fathers, relatives, or friends, in many cases, an individual's first choker setting job represents his initiation into the occupation. As a neophyte to logging, a first-time choker setter is usually subjected to fairly intense socialization by the crew. He is watched for signs of physical weakness or lack of endurance. More important than initial physical endurance however, is the individual's willingness to work up to his full physical capacity without complaint. It is a truism that a willing worker can build up his physical endurance in a matter of days or weeks, but that an unwilling worker is a hopeless case.

The novice logger is made the butt of practical jokes to test his sense of humor. It is not unusual for a new choker setter to be sent to look for a "left-handed" choker only to return from the futile search to find his lunch box welded together or dirt in his sandwiches. If the new crew member is well liked, the initiation is usually carried out in good humor. If he responds appropriately, he goes a long way toward acceptance by the crew. If, on the other hand, the individual is not well liked or responds with anger or defensiveness to the initiation process, the experience can become very unpleasant even to the point of driving him from the crew.

As part of initiation to his job, the new choker setter is expected to very quickly learn the language of logging. For example, he must know what it means to "get out of the bight", to "take a bonus log" or to put a "swede" or "bridle" on a log. If the terminology and appropriate behavior are not learned in short order, the individual acquires the dread reputation of having "no common sense". It is well accepted that a person cannot be a logger without common sense. A new choker setter who learns the job, demonstrates willingness and the ability to carry it out, and avoids acting like a "smart mouth" or "know-it-all" is accepted into the fold in a matter of weeks. His personal lifestyle or his views on religion or politics have far less bearing on his group membership than do his willingness and ability to work.[3] If he is educated, he is expected to overcome the education and demonstrate the common sense required for the job. As was noted above, choker setting is an entry level and usually a young man's job. Occasionally an individual will stay with choker setting for his entire career, but most find it difficult to maintain the speed and agility required as they get older. Most choker setters who choose to stay in logging attempt to move to another job by age 25 or 30.

Landing chasers (knot bumpers) are usually considered by their co-workers to be a step above choker setters in status. The chaser's job is to unhook the chokers from the logs as they are brought to the landing, to trim off any remaining knots or branches and to brand each log with a branding hammer and a can of spray paint. Chasers are usually former choker setters who, for some reason, have not graduated to equipment operator. Their hourly wage is usually only slightly higher than that of a choker setter. In some cases, chasers are young individuals waiting for a better slot to open, but many have reached the end of their career ladder.

It is not uncommon to find a sixty-year-old chaser who has held that position (often with several different employers) for than thirty years.

Cat skinners and skidder operators[4] occupy a status position above that of choker setters and chasers and are usually paid a dollar or two per hour more. Individuals usually acquire the rudimentary skills of cat skinning through informal means. Typically, a choker setter who expresses interest is allowed to occasionally operate the cat on level ground during slack periods. Later he is allowed to tackle steeper terrain. As he learns more he may be allowed to substitute for an operator who is sick or injured. If a cat skinning position opens on the crew, he may be given a one or two day trial. If he fails, he normally is given back his former job and may be allowed to try it again after acquiring more experience. In the case of company operations, union rules usually dictate that the individual with the highest seniority be given the first opportunity to move up.

The machine used to place logs onto trucks is known simply as the loader. The loader operator usually occupies the highest status position on a cat site. He is paid more than cat skinners, and he is often the siderod. Although the rudiments of running a loader are fairly simple, efficient and safe loading is a highly developed skill. A small error can result in a log dropped or slammed against a truck or against worker on the landing. An improperly loaded truck can result in a potentially fatal accident. A slow loader operator can back up trucks waiting to be loaded, which results in the landing being overcrowded with logs.

Loader operating skills are usually acquired by the same type of informal procedure as that described above for cat skinning. An operator may allow the chaser to try his hand during a slack period. An ambitious individual who appeared on the landing before the operator in the morning, or volunteered to "put on a couple of loads" during the lunch break, might also gain valuable experience. Loader operation is such a highly desirable craft that accomplished operators are perhaps the most marketable of all loggers.[5]

The role of the siderod can be compared to the popular stereotype of the army master sergeant. He typically has no more education or formal training than anyone else on the crew and, in many cases, a number of the younger crew members may be better educated. The siderod has come up through the ranks having experience in nearly every job on the crew. In addition, he has probably acquired a considerable repertoire of mechanical skills over the years, which enables him to make minor and, in some instances, major equipment repairs. In short, he is an all around logger. The siderod usually has the power to dismiss crew members, although he may or may not have hiring privileges. In any case, he has considerable influence with respect to who is hired. Company siderods are usually constrained by union regulations from firing crewmen, but they can recommend to the company that an individual be terminated. Union contracts normally provide tenure protection for workers who have passed a one- or two-month probation period so that formal procedures, including hearings, must be followed to fire a worker. In such instances, the siderod is required to play the role of prosecuting attorney.

All of the siderod's duties are tied to one major responsibility: to see that a sufficient volume of logs is produced. It is his job to quickly deal with any obstacles to production that may occur and to get the logs moving again. In smaller gyppo operations the owner may be present full or part-time on the job thus eliminating the need for a siderod. In instances where the owner is present part of the time, there may be no formal designation with respect to who is in charge in his absence. In such cases, an unstated understanding is usually reached, and one of the older, more experienced crewmen is designated as the decision maker. The responsibility of leadership falls most frequently on the individual with whom the owner normally leaves instructions upon his departure.

A number of technological developments occurred in the years between the two studies, and these appear to impact crew configurations on cat sides in areas where they have been adopted. One is the adaptation of the feller buncher from use in the southeast U.S. to employment in second-growth Douglas-fir stands. The feller buncher is a large, track mounted device with curved metal "arms", which are wrapped around a tree to stabilize it while a rotary saw or large shears sever the tree at ground level. Feller bunchers are typically used with rubber tired skidders mounted with mechanical grapples in place of chokers. Trees are piled by the feller buncher and picked up by the grapples for transport to the landing. Although no feller bunchers were observed by fieldworkers during the impact study, Roberge (1991) reports that they can currently be used for trees up to twenty inches in diameter, thus allowing the elimination of both choker setters and fallers. The limitations appear to be the need for small diameter trees and relatively flat ground. Another recent innovation is the computer-equipped delimbing head used on the landing. The loader operator feeds logs into the device, so that remaining branches are removed and cut to length prior to loading.

Yarder Sides

A considerable percentage of standing timber in the West is located on terrain that is simply too steep or rocky to safely and productively log with cats, skidders, or feller bunchers. Although helicopters have come into use in rough terrain logging in the last twenty years, the majority of such work is carried out by the use of yarders. A yarder (high lead side) utilizes a system of cables and blocks (pulleys) in conjunction with a machine called a yarder to move logs to the landing. (The yarder is the technological descendant of the old-time steam donkey described in the previous chapter.) A detachable boom has replaced the spar tree, and the cable and guy line system has become more intricate. There are actually several classes of modern yarders, including the European *Wissen* model, that move logs particularly long distances, downhill. However, the crew configuration is fairly consistent across all types. The more difficult terrain and the machinery involved combine to make yarder logging a more physically difficulty and dangerous proposition than is the case for working with cats. It also requires more intensive teamwork by the crew.

After the trees have been felled, bucked, and limbed by the fallers, and the crew has set up the yarder and accompanying cable rigging, two or more choker setters and a rigging slinger take their places among the logs to be yarded. Most yarders are placed uphill and, in some cases, out of direct line of sight from the logs to be moved. The rigging slinger carries a specially designed portable radio transmitter called a "talkie tooter" that allows him direct contact with the yarder operator. In addition to voice contact, which is rarely used due to the problem of background noise from the machinery, the talkie tooter allows the rigging slinger to signal the yarder operator by means of a code consisting of different length blasts on a horn.

A metal carriage, to which several chokers are attached, is lowered down the main line of the rigging. The carriage is stopped upon the signal from the rigging slinger, at which point the line is slacked, allowing the chokers to be detached. The choker setters quickly set chokers on logs chosen by the rigging slinger and reattach chokers to the carriage. The three workers are then obliged to run a safe distance out of the way of potential rolling logs, rocks, or flying debris. Once they are clear, the signal is given to the yarder operator to take up the slack, and then, if all is well with the set, to move the logs up the hill. When the logs reach the landing, the chokers are removed by the chaser and the process repeats itself.

Space here does not permit a description of the dozens of kinds of accidents that can result in injuring or death to yarder crewmen. The most constant danger is that of logs or debris rolling on top of the choker setters and rigging slinger. The steep terrain and presence of logs and brush make fast movement difficult for them despite their caulk (hob-nailed) boots. A hard hat affords little protection from a several thousand pound rolling log. Another ever present danger is that a portion of rigging under high tension will suddenly snap and fly at a high rate of speed in an unpredictable direction. Nearly every yarder crewman interviewed or encountered had stories to tell of diving behind a stump while a log or chunk of debris passed narrowly over his head or of having to duck flying rigging. Accounts concerning fatalities are very common occupy the bottom rungs of the status hierarchy on a yarder side. The rigging slinger is a step above them. In order to achieve that position, an individual is required to have several seasons of successful choker setting and to have demonstrated good judgment. He and the yarder operator carry the responsibility for the safety of the entire crew. A serious error in judgment by either of them would likely result in demotion or dismissal, or at the very least, strong informal sanctioning by the crew.

The yarder and loader operators occupy approximately equal status positions and command about the same rate of pay. The high status position of the equipment operators is shared to a degree at least by the hook tender, or hooker as he is often called. The hooker is responsible for making decisions concerning the set up of the yarder and for rigging each area to be logged. He chooses the site for the yarder and the trees to which the rigging is to be attached. The hooker usually works one strip ahead of the crew attaching blocks to stumps and trees, falling trees, and clearing brush that would interfere with the rigging. In addition to this high level of responsibility, the hooker's job is physically quite demanding. He is required to carry hundred pound blocks on his back and to pull heavy cable long distances through rough terrain. A hooker normally has several years of choker setting and rigging slinging experience in his background. Heavy equipment operation experience is not usually a prerequisite for the job, although reasonable competence in falling is necessary.

Yarder crews tend to develop a higher level of cohesion than is true for cat logging crews. A cat skinner and choker setter pair need to work closely together, but tend to function quite independently of other pairs skidding to the same landing. They are usually left alone by the siderod so long as their production level is adequate and they clean up all the logs behind them. The nature of the technology forces yarder crews to work more closely together. If one choker setter or landing chaser is slow, the pace of the entire side is reduced. The yarder operator can push the crew beyond comfortable or even safe limits by running the yarder in an overly aggressive manner. One yarder operator described at some length the care to which he goes to maintain a balance between adequate production and the safety and comfort of the men in the brush. He stated that an operator who pushes too hard creates tension and anxiety, and in extreme cases, hostility on the part of the crew.

Roberge (1991) reports that in British Columbia, yarder sides are currently being equipped with grapples which are lowered over cut timber on the rigging. He states that the yarder operator, who often cannot see the logs, is directed by a worker known as a spotter. The spotter provides directions by means of signals transmitted over a radio similar to a talkie tooter. This arrangement allows for the elimination of one of the most dangerous jobs in logging, high lead choker setting. This innovation does not appear to have made significant inroads in the United States as of this writing.

Helicopter Sides

The third type of logging system commonly found in the West utilizes helicopters to move logs from the stump to the landing. Although by conventional logging standards helicopter logging is still in its infancy, it is of particular interest here because it has introduced some dramatic changes in the logger's work world is organized. In both cat and yarder logging, individuals who make it to the top of the status ladder (i.e., siderods, hookers, and heavy equipment operators) almost invariably start at the bottom. The elite of helicopter logging are pilots, or co-pilots; below them are aviation mechanics who service the helicopters.

While logging crew members have typically developed their skills (including mechanical knowledge) through informal instruction and experience, aviation people have extensive formal technical training. They speak a technical language and follow formal aviation procedures that are foreign to the loggers' informal, but tradition-bound, world. Most aviation people involved in logging have military backgrounds, and most pilots are former officers. One pilot described at length the difficult period of adjustment between the rigging crew and the aviation people that occurred when his company began helicopter logging. Owing to their former status as military officers, pilots were accustomed to giving orders to those around them. Thus they attempted to "call the shots" from the air during logging. After a trial period, the rigging crew convinced them that the operation would proceed more efficiently and safely if a crewman on the ground had responsibility for signaling the pilot in much the same way a rigging slinger signals a yarder operator.

Despite concessions that have been made, aviation people, particularly the pilots, clearly exert authority vis-a-vis the rigging crew. The pilot determines whether or not conditions are right to fly and thereby decides whether or not the crew will work on a particular day. The pilot also has the last word with respect to procedures that involve the helicopter. A rigging crewman can rarely expect to win an argument with a pilot. The aviation crew has the right to call a safety meeting at any time to remind rigging crewmen about safety procedures in connection with the operation.

The lowest paid choker setter and the siderod on a traditional logging operation may have a salary differential of only thirty- to thirty-five percent. Pilots and co-pilots, on the other hand, often command salaries up to several times that of the best paid rigging crewman. Additionally, pilots and co-pilots are usually in a rotation that requires them to work about half the number of hours put in by the rigging crew. Aviation mechanics are also very well paid, although their hours tend to be long. The boundary between loggers and aviation people is evidenced by the patterns of tents and camp trailers established when the crew is forced to camp on the job. Both aviation people and loggers commented that the two groups nearly always form separate camps within the area designated as the campsite.

The configuration of a helicopter rigging crew is somewhat different from that on a yarder site. The lowest status members are choker coilers who have the strenuous but monotonous duty of coiling and assembling bundles of chokers to be transported by helicopter to the woods crew. Choker coilers are not ordinarily considered to be full-fledged loggers. They are often casual laborers who move in and out of various occupations. As a helicopter crew moves from state to state following the work throughout the year, the majority of its members go along. Choker coilers, and in some cases, choker setters, are typically hired in the local community on a temporary basis. However, a choker coiling job can be used as a means of entering into the mainstream of the occupation.

Owing to the expense involved in running a helicopter, there are usually two sides, but only one active landing, per operation. A side, in this context, consists of two choker setters, a hooker, and a strip runner. The two sides are usually located at least one hundred yards apart, though each is within one minute of flying time from the landing. The helicopter alternates, taking a turn of logs from each side. The objective of this arrangement is to make optimal use of every minute of the ship's expensive flying time, so that it never hovers idly while a turn is being prepared. A second helicopter, much smaller and less expensive to run, is used on all but the smallest of operations to fly chokers back to the two sides.

The strip runner has the highest status on each side. His responsibility is to lay out the pattern of the turns so that the flying time is used efficiently. He is also charged with locating any missed logs. The hooker's job is equivalent to that of the rigging slinger on a yarder side. The helicopter is equipped with a length of cable to which a hook with an electronically controlled release is attached. The hooker, who is equipped with a length of cable to which a hook with an electronically controlled release is attached. The hooker, also equipped with a portable "two way" radio, guides the ship to a position directly above the logs to be taken and hooks up the pre-set chokers. An important part of his responsibility is to accurately estimate the weight of the logs to be lifted. If he underloads the ship, efficiency is lost; if he overloads it, the ship could be pulled from the air. The helicopter is equipped with an internal scale, monitored by the co-pilot, as the turn of logs is lifted. If the safe weight load maximum is exceeded, the hook release is activated and the logs are dropped.

The chokers setter's job is roughly equivalent to that of his yarder side counterpart, except that the helicopter choker setter often has the opportunity to set several turns ahead, thus relieving immediate pressure. If a helicopter side were to fall behind in choker setting, its crew would be under considerably more pressure than would be the case on a yarder side. Choker setting is considered a much more desirable job than is choker coiling. Choker coilers who intend to stay in the occupation usually attempt to move up to choker setting at the first opportunity. Landing chasers and loader operators have the same responsibilities and occupy roughly the same status positions as their counterparts on cat or yarder sides.

Internal Boundaries--Center and Periphery

Rigging crew members, together with fallers, look upon themselves as the core of the occupation. Road builders and truck drivers are seen by fallers and riggers as loggers, but loggers of a more peripheral type. Rigging crewmen and fallers perceive themselves as the "center of it all," the "real loggers" as it were. For example, truck drivers are often ridiculed behind their backs (and occasionally to their faces) by woods loggers as being chronic complainers who have a "soft job" as compared to the men who work in the woods. In this sense, falling and skidding of logs is seen to be the "core" set of activities of logging, while road building and truck driving are seen as necessary, but somehow secondary, components of the process.

Indication of the boundary between road builders and rigging crewmen was uncovered during interviews of several individuals who had worked for a large company that employed both types of crews. A number of interviewees volunteered comments about the differences between the two groups. In this particular case, road builders and riggers had separate crew busses for transportation from the company yard to the woods. When the crews arrived for work in the morning, the road builders would invariably gather on one side of the yard and the rigging crew on the other. There would often be quite lively inter-group conversation, but very little interchange between groups. One road builder commented that one look at the appearance of the workers in the two groups would serve to distinguish them. Road builders, by his account, took better care of their work clothes, while those of the rigging crew "resembled a garbage dump."[6]

Rigging crewmen tend to become specialized within a particular logging system. For example, an individual setting chokers on a cat side is more likely to move to cat skinning than he is to move to choker setting on a yarder side. This phenomenon seems to have at least as much to do with labeling, both self labeling and that done by peers and employers, as it does to any obstacle inherent in the job requirements. A common sentiment expressed by informants was that less effort is required to stay with a particular type of logging than to switch systems. This is, of course, less true for landing chasers and loader operators whose jobs are very similar in all three systems.

The other side of this coin is the potential employer's impressions. An employer who is hiring choker setters for a yarder side is likely to prefer an applicant with yarder experience. The rationale would be that the individual with only cat experience might require a few days "break in" period and might discover that he prefers to go back to cat logging. The result of this preference is that each system tends to develop its own group of workers who may change employers, but who less often switch technologies. Although helicopter logging is a fairly recent phenomenon, helicopter loggers are coming to view themselves as a highly specialized group. As helicopter logging becomes increasingly prevalent, it seems likely that this specialization will continue.

Road Builders

A third major category in the loggers' social organization is road builders. As the name implies, the road builder's task is to construct logging roads into places where timber harvest is to take place. The first task in road building is to remove trees in the path of the intended road. Once the projected road has been marked with stakes by surveyors, right-of-way fallers move in to fall the necessary trees. Right-of-way falling is not highly productive in terms of wood volume, hence, the fallers are usually paid by the day rather than on a volume basis. Nonetheless, their pay is usually the highest of anyone on the road crew with the exception of the foreman.

Each road crew has at least one cat for skidding logs (referred to as a skid cat to distinguish it from the usually larger road-building bulldozers), a cat skinner, and one or two choker setters. There are often one or more manual laborers on the crew; these laborers are responsible for pick and shovel work in the installation of culverts to channel water from streams that are traversed by the road. Often college students on summer vacation or casual laborers, laborers are not ordinarily full-fledged members of the occupational group, but, like choker coilers on a helicopter crew, some use it as a means to enter logging. Choker setters and skid cat skinners constitute the next level up the hierarchy. Some choker setters eventually become skid cat skinners, and cat skinners occasionally move up to running road building dozers or other heavy equipment.

The three types of heavy equipment most commonly used in actual road construction are bulldozers (called "dozers"), road graders, and scrapers. The reader may already be familiar with the appearance of a bulldozer and a grader. A scraper is a machine about the size and shape of a steam roller. It is equipped with a blade which "scrapes up" large quantities of soil and loose rock. The material is fed into the "belly" of the machine, which can be later opened to dump the load. There is no particular status difference between the operators of these machines. An operator is more valuable to the crew if he can operate two or three of them.

After the right-of-way logs are skidded, a dozer operator moves in to carry out the pioneering work. This consists of using the blade to remove stumps, rocks, and other obstacles, as well as cutting the sides of steep bands and changing the grade of the road where that is necessary. In instances where large quantities of materials are to be moved or in some cases imported by truck from another location, the scraper is utilized. When this work is completed, the finish work is carried out with a dozer. Finish work amounts to smoothing out the road surface, cleaning up the edges, and making final adjustments in the cut banks in preparation for the final touches by the grader.

Equipment operation skills are acquired in the same manner as on a rigging crew. An individual with potential may be given a few opportunities to learn to run a piece of equipment. If an absence or opening on the crew occurs, he may be given a short trial. It is fairly common for a skid cat skinner who has opportunities to observe dozer operators doing blade work to eventually move into a dozer operation job. Road crew foremen occupy positions analogous to siderods on rigging crews. They are responsible for the quantity of the crew's daily work. In gyppo operations, the foreman may also be an equipment operator. Road crew foremen typically have the knowledge to run any piece of equipment on the job.

Although road builders recognize and take pride in the fact that the roads they build are a vital link in getting the logs to town, they also value the quality and appearance of the roads themselves. They are often required to work in terrain so difficult that it is often a major accomplishment to put in the road at all. An aesthetically pleasing as well as functional product in such a situation is a source of considerable job satisfaction. Many complain that rigging crews are careless in their treatment of roads. One road builder commented that it is so distressing to watch a rigging crew "tear up" a newly completed road, that he prefers to move to a new location before the rigging crew move in.

Log Truck Drivers

The final category within the occupation is that of log truck drivers. The driver's job is among the least physically demanding in the occupation, but he usually works the longest hours. Drivers hauling from a given side establish a rotation by which each takes a turn at receiving the first load of the day. The driver who is "first out" on a given day is ordinarily "last out" the following day and is worked one slot up the list each successive day. In the summer months the first truck may be loaded at five a.m. or earlier. Depending on the length of the commute involved, the driver who is first out may be required to arise as early as one a.m. Depending on the number of loads he is able to transport in a given day, and the distance to the various mills involved, the driver may not arrive home that evening until eight p.m. or later. The psychic and physical strain resulting from the long hours and loss of sleep is compounded by the driver's inability to predict the length of any given workday.

The log truck driver's position in the loggers' working world is somewhat different than that of the other components described above. Log truck drivers do occasionally refer to themselves as loggers, particularly in the context of distinguishing themselves from highway drivers. However, this use of the term is understood to mean log truck driver and not "woods logger." Few log truckers express any desire to work in the woods. Many have set chokers, and some have heavy equipment operation experience, but few want to go back to the "brush." Log truckers have some affinity with drivers who haul freight on the highways, though they lay claim to being a breed apart from them. Log truckers see themselves as much more highly skilled than highway drivers, particularly with respect to their ability to negotiate difficult logging roads. They take pride in their willingness and ability to drive logging roads regardless of how muddy or icy they may be. (Nearly every driver interviewed, with more than two or three years experience, had been involved in an accident in which the truck he was driving rolled over.)

The group ties among log truckers are strengthened by frequent interaction. While a woods logger may see only the same dozen of his co-workers, and perhaps a few drivers on most days, a trucker may contact forty or fifty of his fellows during his travels on an average workday. Communication is facilitated by the nearly always present Citizens Band radio. Few drivers can resist the temptation to greet another in passing on the road. Useful information concerning job openings, road conditions, directions to a landing or a mill, or the location of police vehicles is passed along on the radio. The C.B. also serves as a key link in a very well developed "underground" among drivers. Tidbits of gossip and rumors travel with startling speed.

There is a common expression among loggers: "If one driver hears something in the morning, they will all know it by nightfall." Drivers are quick to notice a strange driver or truck on the road. The newcomer will almost invariably be contacted on the radio or face to face on the landing or at the mill yard, where he will be asked about his employer, the job he is currently working, and other pertinent facts. Although the questioning is almost always friendly, it is persistent. Log truckers like to know what's going on in their territory.

There is a strong norm among log truckers with respect to mutual aid. If a log truck is broken down on the roadside, it is a breach of etiquette to pass by without stopping or at least making radio contact. Stopping to offer aid can be costly in terms of losing one's place in line on the landing or perhaps even missing a trip. Costs aside however, aid is almost always offered when the broken down truck is a logging truck. One the other hand, broken down highway trucks are usually passed by without even an attempt at radio contact.

There are three categories of ownership with respect to log trucks. Large timber-holding companies own trucks and employ drivers on an hourly basis. The second category is that of large gyppo operators, who often own fifteen or more trucks. In some cases a gyppo logger may own trucks primarily for use on his own harvesting operation. The use of these trucks may contracted out when they are not needed by his own logging sides. Some larger gyppos pay drivers on an hourly basis, but most pay on the basis of volume of wood hauled per unit distance. Truck owners are almost always paid on a volume-distance basis. The third category of truck ownership is that of the small time gyppos who own and operate one or two trucks. With the possible exception of falling, log trucking offers the most ready route to owning one's own means of production in logging. In good economic times, banks have been usually willing to loan an experienced driver the cash necessary to purchase a used truck. If business goes well for a while, the common pattern is for the individual to graduate to a new truck, to buy a second one and hire someone, or to take on a business partner to drive. In difficult economic times, these small time operators are usually the first to lose their equipment to foreclosure. The ranks of wage-earning log truck drivers are replete with individuals who once owned a truck.

When preparing to bid on a job, the truck owner is informed about which species of logs are to be sent to which mills. It is not uncommon for logs from a given job to be sent to five different mills.[7] He will estimate the mileage and time required to haul from the job to each mill and then negotiate prices per unit volume (thousand board feet) for each mill with the logging contractor. These negotiations may be based either on net or gross scale. A trucker who is paid on a gross scale basis is paid for the total volume of wood hauled. If he agrees to haul for a net scale, he is paid only for the amount of usable volume hauled. Thus, if the log scalers at the mill determine that a particular load is thirty percent cull (unusable) the trucker receives payment only on the basis of the remaining seventy percent. The trucker's major frustration in this arrangement is that he has no control over the quality of logs loaded on the truck.

The individual driver, paid on a volume basis, is given incentive to haul additional logs. He also assumes additional risks. If he is delayed at the landing, the mill, or somewhere in between, he absorbs the loss. A truck breakdown that requires a couple of days to repair is particularly disastrous for such a driver. The loader operator has a great deal of power vis a vis the individual driver. There exists a strong norm which holds that drivers are to accept whatever load is given them without complaint. The loader operator's primary objective is to move logs as efficiently as possible from the landing. This is, at times, at cross purposes to the truck driver's desire for a particular load to either maximize his income for a given day, or to get him home that evening at a reasonable hour. Some loader operators allow truck drivers a little negotiating room with respect to loads while others will not.

An example of this was provided by one loader operator who described a situation in which a group of drivers were working a job that required them to live away from home during the week. They traveled home on Friday nights. It was his practice to save a load of cedar (a scarce commodity on that particular job) for each truck for Friday afternoon because the mill which accepted cedar was located in the vicinity of the drivers' home community. This allowed the drivers to arrive home several hours earlier on Friday than would otherwise be possible. When the drivers began to request cedar on other nights, and to quarrel about who received cedar and who did not, the operator became angry and punished the drivers by loading cedar whenever it became available.

The loader operator can affect the driver's paycheck simply by the size and quality of the logs that he loads. The driver is responsible for legal weight limits, and thus can tell the operator to stop loading at any point.[8] Drivers are not, however, ordinarily in the position to demand large logs (which contain higher volume per unit weight). Owing in part, at least, to the awareness that the loader operator can enhance or reduce their paychecks, drivers can often be induced to do "a favor" for the operator or someone on the crew, such as stopping off for a pack of cigarettes on the way back from the mill. Some drivers will take the crew a "gift" of a case of cold beer on a Friday afternoon. In some cases, the beer is freely given, but in other it amounts to something between extortion by the crew and bribery by the driver. A particularly high volume load on a truck is cynically referred to as a "beer load."

Drivers paid on a volume basis can be described as being in a race to haul the highest possible volume of wood to the mill in the shortest possible amount of time. In addition to uncooperative loader operators, poor road conditions, back ups at the mill and landing, mechanical breakdowns and traffic on the highway, the driver has another set of problems with which to contend: traffic laws and their enforcement. States and counties usually have fairly stringent load weight limitations for cargo bearing trucks. Permanent truck scales are set up along some heavily traveled routes. Drivers who haul along such routes rarely overload their trucks, as they are often caught and required to pay a substantial fine. Drivers hauling on out of the way routes are sometimes tempted to allow the truck to be overloaded in the hope of avoiding detection. Drivers point out that if they can avoid detection eighty or ninety percent of the time, their fines will be more than equaled by the extra income from the large loads. Thus, many truckers find themselves in a cat and mouse game with law enforcement officers.

The games become quite personal at times as drivers and police officers come to know each other. In some cases, familiarity works to the driver's advantage. Some officers are willing to "look the other way" in the case of minor infractions by a local driver. Some, however, assume a proprietary attitude with respect to their territory. A driver who antagonizes such an officer can find himself being frequently "written up" for inconsequential infractions.

Conclusion

Fallers and rigging crew members quite clearly constitute the symbolic core of the loggers' working world. If an individual identifies himself as a logger without qualifiers, the investigator's experience would lead to the prediction that he is likely to be a faller or member of a rigging crew. If he is a logging road builder, he is likely to identify himself as such; if he is a logging truck driver, he would be unlikely to refer to himself as simply a logger. As will be seen in Chapter 4, there is considerable variability between the four major categories with respect to how individuals in them are seen by others, as well as how they define themselves and express commitment to the occupation. Nonetheless, members of these four categories perceive themselves as having a world in common. From a sociological point of view, the evidence summarized above suggests that it is valid to "draw a line around" the four subgroups and categorize them as a clearly defined occupational group.[9]

Theoretical/Methodological Note

For the sociologically-minded reader, a brief note should be added. The primary mode of inquiry adopted in these studies was that of the interpretive perspective of the discipline (Burrell and Morgan, 1979; Borman, Compte, and Goetz, 1986; Denzin, 1992). In contrast to more "objectivist" approaches that emphasize measurement of social phenomena and quantification, the interpretive sociologist attempts to understand the world view people construct or adopt to lend coherence to their lives: "As a distinctive qualitative approach to the social, [the interpretive approach] attempts to make the world of lived experiences directly accessible to the reader" (Denzin, 1992: 82).

The specific theoretical perspective relied upon here is that of Symbolic Interactionism (Blumer, 1969; Fine, 1990, 1993). Adopting this perspective means that one begins the research process with the assumption that an empirical world exists that can be understood through study and observation. In Blumer's famous admonition to sociologists:

> The empirical world] stands over against the scientific observer, with a character that has to be dug out and established through observation, study and analysis. This empirical world must forever be the central point of concern. It is the point of departure and the point of return in the case of empirical science. It is the testing ground for any assertions made about the empirical world. "Reality" for empirical science exists only in the empirical world, can be sought only there, and can be verified only then (Blumer, 1969: 21-22).

Blumer argued that to adequately inquire into the complexity of a particular social world, two complementary approaches to study are called for: Exploration and inspection. Exploration is the preliminary step by which the investigator becomes familiar with the social world in question and sharpens and defines the research problem. The exploration process is inductive in that it starts with a broad focus and becomes more sharply defined as the investigator gains knowledge and insight into the dynamics under study. The investigator is enjoined to seek out knowledgeable informants who are "acute observers" of their own social world. Blumer contended that a handful of such individuals can often gain the investigator more knowledge than hundreds of less-than-observant individuals who may collectively comprise a representative sample.

Notes

1. Due to the empirical basis of this study, masculine pronouns are used freely in describing loggers.

2. The term "landing" refers to a relatively small area of ground, immediately adjacent to a logging road, that has been cleared and leveled to allow logging trucks to be turned around and loaded.

3. It should be noted that certain personal characteristics would tend to make the person's acceptance into the group more difficult. A worker who somehow stands out as being different, would likely have to work harder to prove himself, but the ultimate group membership criteria are willingness and ability to do the work. This will be discussed in greater detail below.

4. The positions are interchangeable although cats are somewhat more difficult to operate and are capable of handling steeper ground.

5. A possible exception to this is yarder operators. See below.

6. The author, of course, does not necessarily endorse the value judgments made by this or any other informant. The important point in this discussion is the differences that were perceived to exist between the groups.

7. Any one load of logs is sent to a single mill.

8. Modern log trucks are equipped with internal scales.

9. It should be noted that the studies reported in this volume focus on forest workers for whom the occupation is a way of life. In a classic study conducted in Oregon in the 1970s, labor economist Joe B. Stevens identified a second category of wood products workers: "These are the 'peripheral' workers. [A portion] are college students who work seasonally. Most of the remainder . . . mobile workers, try to keep employed all year but must splice wood products and other jobs together to make a living. Primarily in their twenties and with little seniority at low skill jobs, they are neither committed to nor sought after by wood products employers (Stevens, 1979: 718)." A study of this other category of workers would very likely prove interesting and useful, but such is not the purpose here.

5

The Attributes of the Logger's Social World: Identity, Friendship Patterns, and Shared Reality

As noted in Chapter 1, Van Maanen and Barley (1984) suggest a view of occupational community with four elements: People who regard themselves to be involved in the same sort of work, whose identity is closely tied to that work, who share "values, norms and perspectives" linked to, but extending beyond, the work setting, and whose social relationships "meld the realms of work and leisure." Each of these was found to be present in the case of the loggers observed and interviewed for these studies.

The Logger's Occupational Self

The concept of self is an integral component of any symbolic interactionist analysis. One of the critical tasks of this research was to attempt to discover how central the role identities associated with the logging occupation are to the individual's overall sense of self. It was necessary for this study to look into the social group dimensions of the occupational self. Specifically, it was important to know what particular forms the occupational role identities assumed and how they differed, if at all, among individuals within particular occupational subgroups and also among subgroups.

The investigator went into the field with the expectation that the logger's occupational self would be relatively monolithic and further that the role identity "logger" would tend to be the dominant component in the individual's collection of role identities. Additionally, it was anticipated that the role identities in the individual's repertoire would be a rather narrow set consisting only of those defined by the occupational culture to fit with that of logger. For example, it would be thoroughly appropriate for the logger to possess the role identities of father, husband, deer hunter, and beer drinker, but inappropriate to possess those of ballet dancer, environmentalist, or sociologist. An additional expectation was that the role identity "logger" would supersede any sub category role identities, such as faller or cat skinner, and that the hierarchy built around the role identity of logger, once acquired, would tend to be stable throughout the individual's lifetime. The findings relating to these expectations will be discussed throughout the chapter.

In general, a strong occupational self was found to be very much in evidence among the loggers interviewed and observed. Many treated the possibility of leaving the occupation to be out of the realm of reality. One individual, who had just finished an extended description of how difficult logging was under the current set of market conditions, was particularly adamant on the subject of leaving the occupation. He insisted that there were simply no other suitable occupations available. When factory work was suggested, he ruled that out because it would require moving to a city. Working in a restaurant was eliminated because it required dealing with the public. Working on a state highway crew was deemed unacceptable because it would involve "too many bosses." In the mind of this man, logging represented the only acceptable way to make a living. This individual represents a somewhat extreme example of a very common theme among loggers. For many, particularly rigging crewmen and fallers, logging is so much a part of them that no realistic alternatives are seen. When asked to defend this position, the logger's first response was typically to argue that there are no other job possibilities open in rural areas. When pushed, however, most loggers admit to a high level of emotional involvement in the work. "It gets in your blood" is a common statement.

The self is in evidence most strongly when the logger proudly relates stories of personal experiences in which he, or someone with whom he identifies, is the hero. Fallers frequently relate stories concerning such occurrences as "the tree that fell the wrong way." Most also take great pleasure in describing unusually large trees they have fallen. Nearly every faller remembers the day on which he had the highest production of his career. Rigging crewmen tell similar stories. One cat skinner proudly related how he "got his start on a cat". The siderod, so the story went, "picked up" a turn of logs with a cat, left it on top of a steep hill, and walked back to the landing. The individual, who was a choker setter at the time, was told "if he could bring in the turn of logs, the cat skinning job was his." He was successful, of course, and never tired of relating the story. Log truckers proudly tell stories of hazardous driving on slick, muddy logging roads with shifting loads and of driving nearly around the clock for two or three days at a stretch. Road builders tell about "punching" roads through steep and dangerous terrain and difficult, rocky soil. The stories loggers tell represent more than simple boastfulness. They serve to set the subject of the story (usually the storyteller himself) apart from ordinary people and to define him as someone with extraordinary abilities and courage.

The logger's occupational identity was observed to focus on four interrelated themes: Independence, pride in skill, pride in facing danger, and a sense of being in a unique category of workers. The sense of independence is central to all of this and is particularly pronounced among fallers. As was noted in Chapter 3, fallers are usually independent subcontractors; thus they often claim that they work for no one but themselves. Nearly every faller interviewed listed a number of hardships associated with the job, including inevitable injuries, the high cost of equipment, and the necessity of often having to live away from home. Each of them listed independence, personal freedom, and the lack of a necessity for cooperating closely with others as major reasons for staying with their jobs. Even falling partners rarely work within fifty yards of each other. Each tree to be cut represents a challenge, and fallers derive satisfaction from facing that challenge alone. One faller proudly stated: "Fallers are the renegades. They do their own thing. They're in their own little world. They rarely cooperate except when they work near the landing."

Although rigging crewmen cannot claim the same degree of freedom as fallers in carrying out their jobs, they look on themselves as a very independent lot. Even the relatively low status choker setter values the sense of having his own domain. If he does his job well, he expects to be left alone. Equipment operators generally expect to be granted even more autonomy than that given to choker setters or landing chasers. An experienced cat skinner, for example, expects to be assigned a "patch of ground" from which to skid logs and to be "turned loose" to accomplish his task. An experienced loader operator will ordinarily tolerate very little in the way of guidance or advice from the siderod, fellow crewmen, or truck drivers about his loading technique. Rigging crew members generally resent close supervision. It is not uncommon for a worker to quit a job over a relatively minor difference of opinion with a supervisor. Stories are commonly told describing situations in which entire crews walked off a job over a minor dispute with the siderod. Successful siderods master the fine art of demanding high levels of performance, while avoiding close supervision of their independence-minded charges.

Another means that loggers, and particularly gyppos, use to express independence is their readiness to leave a particular employer. It is a well accepted part of the logging culture that workers move frequently from one job to another. The reasons individuals give for moving vary. Reasons frequently mentioned are a desire for a change in co-workers, scenery, or better pay. A common theme running through these explanations, however, is a desire to avoid any sense of dependence on a particular owner or firm. Logging employees prefer to look on themselves as self-reliant individuals who can sell their services to any of a number of employers. A number of loggers interviewed stated that they would occasionally change jobs for no particular reason other than to assert their independence. Others stated that, while they had not changed jobs frequently, they consciously held open the possibility of such a move.

Pride in Skill

Pride in skill is a recurrent theme in the conversations loggers have with each other and with non occupation members, as well as in the stories they tell. Falling, in particular, is seen as a highly demanding skill. Legends often develop around the exploits of particularly skillful and productive fallers. Crew members, in many cases, look upon "their" fallers or one of their fallers as the "best around". Fallers have good reason to take pride in their skill. Falling is a highly developed art. The common saying among fallers that no two trees are alike is quite true. Each stem to be harvested requires the faller to exercise judgment. An error on his part could create a number of problems, ranging from the tree being dangerously "hung up" in the branches of others still standing, to the tree landing on others already fallen. The latter results in smashed unusable wood. Fallers are required not only to be very precise about the placement of individual trees, but also to develop strategies for falling a number of closely spaced trees to minimize breakage and to maximize the efficiency of the subsequent bucking and skidding operations. All of this is carried out in a manner that conserves time and bodily energy, so the maximum volume of wood is "laid on the ground" in a given day. It is generally accepted that a talented individual would require five years of experience in order to acquire the full set of skills a seasoned faller is expected to possess. Several experienced fallers interviewed stated that a portion of those who make the attempt simply never develop the full complement of skills.

Pride in skill is also a very obvious component in the occupational self of the rigging crewman. This is true even in the case of the relatively low status choker setter. Choker setters like to be known as "good" or "fast" in their jobs, and those who do their job well usually find their positive self image reinforced by other crew members. It was stated to the author on a number of occasions that a cat side choker setter can make a cat skinner look very good or very bad.

Landing chasers take pride in their ability to keep things on the landing running smoothly, while individuals who run equipment look to their operational skills as a source of pride. Loader operators like to be known as smooth and efficient in the saying they "put on a load." Cat skinners typically take pride in their ability to "bring in the logs" no matter how steep or rough the terrain. Cat skinners most highly respected by their peers are those who skillfully and aggressively operate on steep ground. No cat skinning stories are told with more pride than those that involve skidding logs on slopes on which other skinners had been unable or unwilling to go. One former company cat skinner told a story about "rescuing" his boss' cat from a tough spot on a steep slope. His reward was a comment from a co-worker in the crew bus on the way home that evening: "What would we ever do if Clarence got scared on steep ground?"

The yarder operator is no exception to the rule of pride in skill. He is well aware that the productivity of the entire side, and indeed the lives of most of the crew, is largely in his hands. The yarder is the most complex piece of machinery to run on an ordinary side (excluding the helicopter of course), and an operator error as small as throwing the wrong lever or misreading a signal could prove disastrous. Road builders tend to tie their pride in skill to equipment operation. One pioneer dozer operator, for example, proudly told of how several individuals had held his job for a few days, but each had failed to make sufficient progress through the rocky soil on a particular site.

The foreman dropped him off on site the first morning, came back several hours later and stated that he had made more progress in those few hours than the previous operator had made in several days. Log truck drivers like to expound at length on the additional skill their jobs require compared to those of highway drivers. They will regale the willing listener with numerous accounts of successfully negotiating difficult logging roads no highway driver would dare to attempt.

Danger

Danger is an everyday part in the lives of all types of loggers. It is well understood by even the least experienced member of a crew that the potential for injury or death exists each time a chainsaw is started or a turn of logs is hooked up. Although specific dangerous situations are often discussed (usually in terms of how the danger can be minimized or the situation avoided), danger in the abstract is rarely a topic of conversation. When asked a direct question concerning danger, a logger will usually acknowledge that it is nearly always "in the back of his mind". In the stoic world of logging, little point is seen in discussing an unpleasant fact of life of which everyone is all too aware.

Living with high danger on a regular basis sets the logger apart in his own mind from other types of workers. The typical reasoning is that the woods is a dangerous place to work, and it takes a particular type of individual to work under such conditions. Logging requires extraordinary alertness and the ability to correctly perceive the nature of a dangerous situation. Loggers must move quickly and decisively in response. Loggers also see their occupation as requiring a good deal of courage or "nerve," because, though it is important to be alert to danger, it is also necessary to function efficiently in spite of it. Often it was stated that an individual cannot be "scared all the time" and make it as a logger. This point was made clear in an interview with a pair of falling partners who matter-of-factly stated that all fallers expect to be injured from time to time. Each of them had spent time in the hospital as a result of injuries. Occasional injuries are seen as part of the job. A person who wants a safe job "had best work somewhere besides the woods."

Individuals who purposely flirt with danger and get away with it are often highly regarded for that reason by their fellow crew members. Fallers, for example, who work hours beyond the point of fatigue to increase their production, are often rewarded with high esteem and laudatory comments. Cat skinners, who operate on terrain so steep that it puts them in danger of "rolling" the cat, are apt to be highly respected. Courting danger can be taken too far, however. Workers who "tear up" equipment, or worse, unnecessarily injure themselves or other workers, are usually regarded as a menace and are often subject to sanctions from the crew or the employer. For example, a situation was observed in which a yarder operator came dangerously and unnecessarily close to slamming a turn of logs into his landing chaser. The comments from the rest of the crew indicated that this individual had been responsible for several other near misses in the past and was at least partially at fault for the recent death of a choker setter. The owner (in this case the owner of the operation also ran the yarder side) had not been present when these incidents had occurred and was not informed of the operator's culpability. Thus, although the individual received no official sanction, he was treated very coldly by his co-workers for the rest of the working day and during the ride home. Unfortunately, it was impossible for the author to follow-up on the situation. It was, however, clear from the limited observation period that, in endangering other workers' lives, the operator had crossed the line from acceptable to unacceptable behavior. Another situation observed involved a landing chaser who was injured by a log that was unexpectedly kicked out by the track of a cat. The accident was not considered by the crew to be the fault of the cat skinner and was treated as something that could have, in one form or another, happened to any crewman at any time.

In addition to hazards that immediately threaten life and limb, loggers are subject to a number of more gradually occurring health risks. Cat skinners, for example, are subject of constant bouncing and vibration and tend to develop back and kidney ailments. Fallers often develop circulation problems in their hands as a result of grasping the vibrating saw. The condition known as "white fingers" causes particular discomfort during the winter months. All members of the crew are subject to breathing large amounts of dust from the landings and logging roads and thus run a high risk of developing respiratory problems later in life. Most work around constant noise from engines and tend to gradually develop hearing problems as a result.

The threat of sudden traumatic injury, and the virtual certainty of gradually developing health problems, are treated by loggers as a natural and expected part of their day-to-day existence and are part of a litany of reasons why "no sane person would ever want to be a logger." This dual logic allows the logger to place himself in a special category of workers while rationalizing his decision to risk his health.

The occupational self was not found to be universally strong among the loggers studied. Contrary to initial expectations, the investigation did locate a number of loggers who lacked the more typically strong occupational identity. Those closest to the periphery of the logger's symbolic world, i.e., the road builders and truckers, showed considerably more variability in the strength of the occupational self. There were, however, a number of novice rigging crew members who reported that logging is not a satisfying occupation and stated emphatically that they were actively looking for alternative employment. (More acceptable work would be less physically demanding, dirty and dangerous, would not require "camping out", while providing more intellectual challenge and presenting a more secure financial future.)

However, the investigation located very few woods loggers beyond entry level positions who expressed lack of commitment. A plausible interpretation of this finding is that a "weeding" process similar to that described by Holbrook (1954) for a much earlier era occurs in which individuals who are not physically or emotionally suited for logging, but who somehow survived their break-in period, choose to leave. In some cases, these uncommitted individuals state that they never intended to make logging a life's work. Their relationship to the occupation was purely instrumental; that is, their intention was to make some "quick money" and to move on. In other cases, individuals reported entering the occupation with at least a tentative intention of staying, but then discovered that they were unhappy as loggers.

The subgroup observed to have the most variability in strength of occupational identity is that of log truckers. The small time gyppo owner-operators tend to have very strong occupation identification. They take great pride in their driving skill and their willingness and ability to work long hours and "to haul any load anywhere anytime". This enthusiastic attitude is common among employees of larger gyppo operations and companies, but the latter two types of operations also attract individuals who invest very little of their identity in the occupation, and to whom log trucking "is just a job". Some uncommitted log truckers are former urbanites who parleyed truck driving experience into an opportunity to live in a rural area. Others are long time rural dwellers who have worked at a variety of jobs, of which log trucking is only one. It is interesting to note that this lack of commitment is rare among experienced "wood loggers". An explanation often offered by loggers themselves is that no one would put up, for long, with the physical exertion and the dirt of woods logging unless he "had logging in his blood."

It was observed that the uncommitted individuals do not, in any sense, distance themselves from their work roles when performing their jobs or interacting with other loggers. While they do not necessarily keep secret their lack of lifetime commitment, when performing their occupational role, they conform with the prevailing norm of cheerful hard work. The fieldwork uncovered no evidence to indicate that they were less well-liked or accepted by their fellows than was the case for committed workers, so long as they lived up to the behavioral norms of their peers.

The original expectations about the logger's occupational self were largely borne out, except in the case of road builders. While the faller, the rigging crewman and, in a more limited sense, the trucker each refers to himself as a logger, the road crewman is at least as likely to refer to himself as a road builder who plies his trade on logging roads as he is to identify himself as a logger. Though "getting the logs to town" is recognized as the ultimate purpose of the roads, the road builder, in many cases, takes greater pride in the quality of the road itself. Thus, the road builder can be seen to be on the periphery of the logger's world, in contrast to the faller or rigging member.

The initial predictions, outlined in the beginning of the chapter, concerning the existence of a relatively narrow set of role identities in the logger's repertoire were not completely borne out. It was anticipated that an individual wishing to become a part of the logger group would shed, or at least carefully hide, any conflicting role identities in order to gain acceptance and that once a group member, he would only acquire identities deemed appropriate. Instead, there was found to be considerably more diversity in role identities than was expected. Although no interviewees were located who would own up to being ballet dancers, homosexuals, or members of the Sierra Club, loggers were interviewed who laid claim to such "unlogger-like" role identities as hippie, fundamentalist Christian, teetotaler, and actor in the local community theater. Further questioning revealed that the acceptance of seemingly inappropriate role identities is related to the strong norm of individualism. It is believed that an individual has a right "to live his own life as he sees fit", whether or not his lifestyle conforms to anyone's expectations. On the other hand, an individual who exhibits unconventional (by loggers' standards) characteristics is likely to be required to work harder and to demonstrate his ability more thoroughly than would be the case for a conventional individual. In the end, however, it is an individual's work that makes or breaks him as a group member.

It is also the case, however, that over a period of exposure and interaction with loggers, an individual will be subjected to socialization that will reward logger-like role identities, particularly as they relate to on-the-job behavior or are particularly salient to logging. Thus, the individual may be subtly transformed or exhibit what appears to be the observer to be inconsistencies in attitudes and behavior. For example, one well respected logger interviewed had a four year college degree, wore an earring in one ear, read the *Wall Street Journal* and could be described as a liberal in his political views. However, when the subject of the Forest Service was broached, he argued from a very conventional logger viewpoint.

In summary, the loggers observed exhibited evidence of a strong occupational self but there was considerable variability among novices and members of the more peripheral subgroups. Further, the results indicate that the occupational self is not as monolithic as had been anticipated; rather, the strong norm of individualism fosters greater acceptance of a wider range of role identities than had been expected. It bears repeating that central to the logger's sense of self is the feeling of independence that membership in the occupation grants to the individual. The lack of perceived alternatives to logging by many in the occupation is clearly linked to this dimension.

Loggers' "Off Duty" Friendships

The fieldwork was begun with the expectation that loggers would exhibit a strong tendency to choose friends with whom they spend discretionary time from the ranks of the occupation. The reasoning was based on the assumption that loggers as occupational community members would hold a set of values and a shared conception of reality that would result in strong collegial relationships and mutual trust and respect that does not extend to non-loggers. Additionally, it was anticipated that the logger's typical work schedules, with long hours in the summer months and time off in the winter, would put him "out of sync" with the work/leisure schedules of most other people. The field experience indicates that, although loggers do tend to have occupational peers as friends, this tendency is not nearly as clear cut as was anticipated on the basis of other occupational community studies.

One individual, who responded affirmatively to the query of whether his friends were primarily fellow loggers, explained: "Loggers get along better (with each other). They [develop] mutual respect." Another stated that the majority of his friends were other loggers because of mutual interests: "What would a school teacher and I talk about?" When loggers are asked what they do when they get together with their logging friends, the typical response is that they "drink beer and bullshit". It is a common expression that more "logging" is done in bars than out in the woods. The buildings used to house log trucks by the larger gyppo truck owners also serve as gathering places for informal socializing. It was traditional in the first study area for loggers to gather in log truck shops to drink beer on Friday afternoons. Although log truckers predominated at these gatherings, other loggers are welcome and often attend. The men who gather on Friday afternoons have typically worked a fifty- or fifty-five hour week and were very tired. Yet many remain to socialize for several hours.

Truck and chain saw shops also serve as gathering places for loggers during the winter months when most are laid off. Many gatherings occur almost daily. One individual reported that his group of six to ten friends gathered early each weekday morning in a local diner where they drink coffee for several hours. About mid-morning, they adjourned to a truck stop, where they may spend the balance of the day telling stories and passing time. He reported that the gatherings are not restricted to any particular category of logger.

One small community in the initial study area hosts an annual "Community Days" festival. The main events of the festival feature logging skill contests. The annual gathering draws loggers and their families from a fifty-mile radius. Loggers typically appear in their work clothes ("Hickory" shirts, "Frisco" jeans cut off at mid-calf, suspenders and boots). They competed in events such as log rolling and log sawing with enthusiasm and good humor. They socialized with their fellow loggers while usually consuming large quantities of beer. The annual County Fair also serves as a gathering place for loggers. They typically occupy the section of the fair's beer garden each evening to "swap stories" and, of course, drink beer. It is interesting to note that loggers from all four categories were observed to mix quite freely at these public gatherings. Whatever boundaries separate them in their work-a-day world seem to be inconsequential during festival times.

Friendships within the occupation serve a purpose beyond meeting the individual's needs for socializing. One interviewee stated: "If I need help of any kind, the first four or five people on my list to call would be loggers." He went on to explain that help could mean anything from a loan to assistance with a project "around the house". It was commonly said in interviews that loggers "are the kind of people who would help anyone in need." That goes especially for fellow loggers and their families.

Despite the tendency of most of the loggers interviewed to include occupational fellows in their circle of friends, and to spend a portion of their spare time with loggers, only a small minority restrict their friendships exclusively to other loggers. This appears to be, in part, related to the nature of small town life. As we have noted, loggers tend to live in small rural communities. They are typically long time residents of these communities and thus develop friendships over the years with individuals from many walks of life. For loggers, membership in the occupational group does not preclude friendships with non-logger local residents. This can be seen sociologically, as an overlay of geographic and occupational community. Often the loggers' spouses and children provide additional ties to the local community. Loggers' friendship ties, in some cases, are tied to other group memberships and interests. Recent high school graduates often remain friends with former classmates. A few interviewees reported church-related friendships. Others reported that they pursue hobbies such as hunting and fishing with both logger and non-logger friends alike.

The Logger's Reference Group: Shared Reality

Due to the logger's strong belief in individualism, direct questions about his reference group are not productive. When asked to name the individuals or type of individuals to whom he looks for guidance in shaping opinions, the logger is apt to be offended. His response is likely to be "No one. I think for myself and I make up my own mind about things." If it is pointed out that his opinions are similar to other loggers, he will typically argue that, if such is the case, it is because the opinion "makes sense," or is based on "common sense".

The extent to which values, beliefs, and a shared reality are held in common is a good indication of the extent to which loggers look to each other as a reference group. Thus, special attention was paid to statements by interviewees that began with phrases such as "A logger thinks . . ." You will never catch a logger doing . . . ." It was found that all four categories of loggers share a distinctive socially constructed reality and beliefs that tend to set them apart from other groups in society. Some of the major themes of that shared reality are discussed here.

Perhaps the most sociologically significant, and certainly the most unexpected result, was that loggers were found to identify with two distinct groups. On the one hand, they identify with the occupation as a whole. They see themselves as a very special category of workers who face a unique set of problems and bring a unique set of skills to their work. In this sense, a logger from southern Oregon feels an affinity with loggers in Alaska. The Oregon or California logger may be personally acquainted with only one Alaskan logger or he may know none. Yet his sense of identity, his reference group, extends, at least in an abstract sense, beyond the range of his personal networks. On the other hand, the logger is embedded in a geographically limited, particularistic network. In most cases he has strong ties to fellow loggers within a fairly limited geographic range. His specific role models tend to be individuals in his local area. His job contacts tend to be geographically limited. Some implications of this finding will be discussed below.

Another often repeated observation made in the course of the investigation was that loggers see their occupation as maligned and embattled. They perceived (well before the spotted owl controversy) that their livelihood and the very existence of their occupation was threatened by political and economic forces outside their control. Not unlike Becker's jazz musicians and Salaman's architects, there is a common perception that the "general public" does not appreciate the importance or the difficulty of their work. It is a truism among loggers that members of the public, particularly urban dwellers, want two-by-fours for building houses, but do not want any trees cut to obtain them. In this sense, loggers see themselves as realists in a naive world.

Loggers (again prior to the owl issue) were found to be sensitive about what they perceive to be their poor image with "the public". They perceived themselves to have an ill-deserved reputation as "rapists of the forest". A number of individuals interviewed talked at considerable length about the public's misperceptions of the logger. They attribute their poor image, in part, to demagoguery by environmentalists. Several loggers in the initial study, and many in the latter one, went so far as to label themselves the "real" or "practical" environmentalists of the world. They claimed that if logging contract inspectors allowed them more latitude in on the ground decision-making, loggers would be able to get the logs out in a more efficient and a less environmentally damaging manner than is the case under currently enforced forest practice regulations: "Environmentalists are one way sons of bitches who take their annual walk in the woods, and then go home to vote against logging."

Not only are environmentalists looked upon as the logger's enemy, they are seen as a powerful elite: "In order to vote in the Sierra Club, you need to have a million dollars. The more money you have; the more votes you get."

Environmentalists are seen to be interlopers in the logger's world who, because they typically make their living some place other than the forest, have no legitimate stake in the political battles they fight over forest land management. Furthermore, environmentalists are believed to have little or no practical knowledge of the forest. The environmentalist's knowledge is thought to be limited to that which can be obtained from books and observations made from "nature trails"; hence, their judgments are seen to have no basis in reality.

As the largest holder of publicly owned commercial forest land in the region, the U.S. Forest Service was looked upon by loggers, particularly in the initial study, as a major force in the ongoing "destruction" of the logger's livelihood. The first statement made in a memorable interview by a logger's wife was the following: "You want to hear about logging? I'll tell you one thing wrong with logging, and that's the Forest Service. . . . When the Forest Service gets authority, they try to play God."

Not all loggers expressed quite that depth of feeling for the Forest Service, but some form of negative evaluation of the agency was expressed by nearly every logger interviewed. Opinions ranged from those who saw the Service as a group of people who are forced by "the system" to enforce impractical rules to those who compare it to the German Gestapo. It was often stated that while the Forest Service has always been something of an adversary to the logger, it was relatively benign in its supervision of timber sales on the National Forests until environmental legislation began to be passed by Congress in the mid-1960's. Since that time, the agency has become progressively "tougher" and more "unreasonable" and "impractical" in logging practice regulations from the logger's view. Some loggers claimed that the Forest Service has "gone over to the environmentalists," while others felt that it is the unwilling political prisoner of environmental groups. There was common agreement that in any case the agency is a major factor in making the loggers' life more difficult than it has been in years.

This sentiment was very similar to that recorded earlier by Williamson among north Idaho gyppo loggers:

> Generally, gyppos dislike Forest Service regulations and practices because they feel they restrict the availability of timber and set too many rigid standards governing logging on this land. They express hostility toward District Rangers who manage timber sale programs in each of the ranger districts and who enforce regulations and guidelines governing logging . . . Resentful gyppos describe District Rangers as "little dictators" because their actions and decisions have an enormous impact on the well-being of the population living within their districts. The enforcement of logging restrictions frequently requires interpretations and judgmental decisions on the part of the District Ranger. Gyppos complain that rangers 'follow the book' too closely in enforcing these rules and lack the practical experience and woods knowledge that they, the gyppos have (Williamson, 1976: 146).

The loggers' views of environmentalists are well publicized in the press and came as no particular surprise to this investigation. The depth of resentment toward the Forest Service, however, was unanticipated. The agency, after all, has until recently been charged with maintaining a policy of ensuring a sustained yield of wood fiber from the national forests. As we have noted above and will discuss at greater length below, that policy is currently changing, particularly in the owl forests. The widespread resentment on the part of the group of people (even during the pre-owl controversy period) for a government agency which has the group's long-term well-being as a major policy objective is no small irony.

It became clear early in the initial study that negative evaluation of the agency serves as an important unifying theme for loggers. One logger candidly stated, "I'm a logger, so I'm supposed to hate the Forest Service." Careful attention was therefore given to the reasons loggers gave to justify their evaluation of the agency. This attention served not only to shed light on underlying reasons for Logger/Forest Service conflict, but also yielded more general information about the logger's distinctive world view.

One reason for the logger's resentment of the Forest Service is that the agency's logging practice regulations are typically more stringent than those that apply to private forest land holdings. Although most western states have enacted forest practice legislation over the past two decades that apply to privately owned and state-managed forest land, those that apply to the National Forests are among the most demanding and expensive from the logger's point of view. Although a detailed discussion of federal and state forest practice legislation and regulation is beyond our purpose here, some examples from the logger's point of view may be useful as an illustration. Many Forest Service logging contracts had for many years specified that all logging slash (waste material) and debris be piled for burning or buried on the site[1], while contracts pertaining to forest industry land usually require only that slash be lopped (cut up) and dispersed evenly on the forest floor. Slash disposal is expensive and from the logger's point of view, unrewarding work. Many loggers complained that the Forest Service is often unreasonably strict about the protection of reproduction (young trees) during a harvesting operation. The agency is well known for setting strict requirements about fire fighting and prevention equipment on logging jobs. Several fallers interviewed stated that agency contract inspectors instructed them not only to have a shovel and fire extinguisher present on the site, but to carry them to the base of each tree to be cut. Fallers object to this requirement because they are usually already "overloaded" with a saw, saw files, extra chain, gasoline, oil, and falling wedges.

Loggers' resentment of the Forest Service runs far deeper, however, than agency logging practice regulations. One key to understanding this dynamic is the realization that loggers see themselves as rugged individualists, in both the philosophical and physical sense of that term, who survive and prosper based on individual productive effort and ability. As such, they have respect for the entrepreneur in particular and private enterprise in general, and corresponding disdain for nearly all governmental institutions. To the logger, a worker does not earn his keep unless he produces a tangible good or service with economically quantifiable value. The individual who regulates, or in any way interferes with, an economically productive activity is typically viewed with cynicism or disdain. The government is viewed generally by loggers not only as a nonproductive institution, but one which usually hinders production while taking away a citizen's hard earned dollars and freedom of choice through taxation.

An example of this attitude is the logger's common disdain for O.S.H.A. (Occupational Health and Safety Administration) safety regulations, which are designed to provide for his safety. Government mandated safety devices such as chain breaks for chain saws, or chaps to be worn to protect a faller's shins from the saw, are commonly ridiculed. The investigator has observed entire logging crews whose members refused to wear hard hats unless an O.S.H.A. or company inspection was expected.

Another striking example of the logger's views about the legitimacy of public versus private institutions was the lack of any expressed resentment when a large forest products company in the first study area closed down its mill and harvesting operations and offered them for sale.

The move threw several hundred loggers out of work during a time when logging jobs were more scarce in the area than at any other time since the Great Depression. Several of the loggers who had lost their jobs as a result of the shutdown were of the opinion that the company had secretly planned the closure as long as ten years in advance. Yet, neither they nor anyone else interviewed felt that the company was not entirely within its rights to cease operations without advance notice. The typical explanation was that the company, after all, had provided jobs for a great many years. Now that it was no longer profitable to provide those jobs, the company had every right to cease local operations and concentrate its activities in regions of the country where growing wood is more profitable. It is very likely, however, that any action by a government agency (whether or not it was related to an endangered species) that suddenly threw several hundred loggers out of work would evoke a great deal of hostility.

Another factor in the resentment of the Forest Service is the logger's mistrust of abstract knowledge or rules. Virtually the only legitimate knowledge in the logger's world is obtained through hands-on experience. They deeply resent "being told what to do" by a college trained forester who may never have set a choker or bumped a knot. They resent even more being ordered to carry out a procedure simply because there is a regulation that requires it. As several authors have pointed out (Lee, 1977; Kaufman, 1967), the Forest Service is, in many ways, a classic Weberian rule-oriented organization. Thus, when a Forest Service employee appears on a logging landing, there often occurs what can be best described as a clash of occupational cultures. The Forest Service employee has been told to follow and enforce the rules, while the logger has been socialized to disdain them.

In a broader sense, the Forest Service is symbolic to the logger of much of what has gone "wrong" in his world. Many of the social and political changes that have occurred over the past decades are threatening and frightening to him. The era of heroic individuals battling nothing but the elements to "bring the big logs to town" has given way to a very different time, a time of government regulations, a time when powerful elements of society are questioning whether indeed all those logs should be brought to town. To the logger, the Forest Service represents, in many cases, the front lines, the enforcers of political and social changes. When a Forest Service archaeologist persuades a timber sale administrator to reconsider offering a timber sale because of the presence of significant archaeological artifacts on the site, or when a timber sale is canceled because of the presence of peregrine falcons, the logger sees not only his paycheck being threatened, but there is also a challenge to his basic values. Getting the logs to town is more than a way to make a living; it represents a moral imperative. It Is not surprising that the logger becomes angry or hostile when his generations-old value system is called into question.

Conclusion

The notion of occupational community implies a perceived separateness on the part of members, a sense that they are somehow different from others. As Salaman (1974: 24) states, their "separate world" is a "mental world composed of assumptions, attitudes, knowledge, expectations and shared history." In order for a separate world to exist, occupants must look to each other for reinforcement of the socially constructed reality. With respect to issues salient to the community, other members must compose the individual's reference group. New members must be socialized, and the norms must be constantly reinforced if the cohesiveness of the community is to be maintained.

A question that this research set out to answer is whether or not the logger's social organizations fits these criteria. The answer to that question based on the interpretation of the data presented here is a resounding yes. The loggers observed and interviewed for this research clearly see themselves as a group set apart from the rest of society. Their world, diffuse as it is, does have discernible boundaries, though the work culture and occupational identity follow the individual into his personal life. The logger has a distinctive sense of self and conception of reality that sets him apart from others.

Yet, the community is loose-knit with significant divisions between segments and tensions between occupants of certain work roles. There is significantly more tolerance of behavior and lifestyle than one would expect to find in a tightly knit community. It is ironic that the theme of individualism which serves to unite the diverse elements of the community also serves as a major impediment to development of tighter knit social organization even in a time of external threats. This sense of individualism, coupled with the ideal of personal freedom and independence, is a powerful influence in the loggers' social world and an important part of the commonly held occupational identity. For many, logging is seen as the only way to express this freedom and independence. Other occupations are seen as too structured and constraining. Given this view, it is small wonder that loggers feel threatened and become angry when they perceive that their way of life is threatened.

Notes

1. Recently, this practice has changed somewhat in line with an approach to forest management known as "New Forestry" which advocates leaving more organic material scattered on the site. One can imagine that these new practices may be greeted with cynicism by many loggers given the history of their relationships with "government foresters".

6

Finding Work

Introduction

The present chapter concerns two related aspects of the logger's working world. One of these is how individual loggers go about obtaining work. More specifically, we examine the nature of the information channels or networks through which information is passed concerning the availability of work on the one hand, and, more to the point, the availability and reputation of individuals to do the work. Secondly, we look at the geographic range of the logger's networks as it relates to his ability to find work in areas other than those immediately around his home community.

The reasons for focusing on these particular aspects of the loggers world are three-fold. First, as we have seen, the boundaries of the occupational community are defined largely on the basis of jobs and job functions. One must be (or have been) a logger to be a member of the occupational community. Thus getting one's first logging job represents an important early step in one's recruitment into the occupational community. An understanding of this is critical to understanding the community itself. The second reason for this focus is that the discovery was made in the course of the fieldwork that the occupational community plays an important role in matching experienced workers with jobs. Thus this discussion is aimed, in part, to demonstrate that the loggers' occupational community is not merely an abstract concept, but rather it plays very important practical role in the daily life of its members. The third reason for focusing on "getting a job" in logging is that the process is highly relevant from a policy standpoint. A major theme in the debate over the allocation of forest resources is the effect on forest product jobs. How and where loggers go about obtaining jobs is very relevant to the question of their adaptability to changes in the allocation and timing of forest resource allocation.

There exist substantial bodies of literature in both sociology and economics that are addressed to the question of how workers and jobs come to be matched. Granovetter succinctly characterizes the approach market economics takes to this subject:

> In the classical conception, labor is a commodity, like wheat or shoes, and is hence subject to market analysis: employers are buyers, and employees the sellers of labor. Wages (or in more refined formulations, the total benefits accruing to a worker by virtue of holding a given job) are analogized to price. Supply and demand operate in the usual way to establish equilibrium. The price of labor fluctuates in the short run until that single price is arrived at which clears the market. For homogeneous work, wage dispersion and unemployment are not possible; firms paying more than the equilibrium price for labor will thereby attract workers from firms paying less. This excess of supply over demand will drive down the price. Firms losing employees will similarly be constrained to raise wages. Workers unemployed in the short run may bid for work, driving down wages to the point where they, and those currently working, will all be employed at the new, lower equilibrium wage. This elegant package ties together wages, unemployment, and labor mobility (Granovetter, 1976: 25).

Granovetter's discussion goes on to state that there are several flaws in this conception:

> Several factors militate against perfect labor markets. Inertia as well as social and institutional pressures exert constraints on the free movement of labor contemplated in economic theory . . . Union agreement and community constraints discourage employers from adjusting wages to meet supply and demand . . *The factor most relevant to the present discussion is imperfection of information* (Granovetter, 1976: 26, emphasis added).

In order for a match to occur, the willing buyer (the employer) and the willing seller (the laborer) must be aware of each other's existence and willingness to trade. Anyone who has ever searched for a job or for an employee is aware that exchanging information with potential trading partners is a problematic and energy consuming process. This is evidenced in the corporate world by the existence of highly paid "head hunters" whose sole function is to find suitable prospective employees for companies.

In an attempt to model how prospective employees actually find jobs, Granovetter (1974) carried out a sociological study of male white collar workers in a suburb of Boston. His focus was on the nature of the information channels that individuals utilized in successfully locating a job. He found that individuals in his sample tended to find employment through personal contacts rather than through formal institutionalized procedures. His findings further indicate that job information tends to pass through several interpersonal linkages, and that the individuals who serve as information sources tend to be merely acquaintances rather than close friends of the job seeker. Granovetter used the phrase "the strength of loose ties" to describe his findings.

One question the studies attempted to address is how, under ordinary circumstances, loggers find work. The ability of a logger to locate employment is, of course, dependent on the state of the forest products economy at a given point in time. It would no doubt, be useful to study the structure of the forest products industry and the adaptations that it has undergone to cope with changes in the national and world economy. Another area relevant to the logger's ability to find employment is related to methods the owners and managers of logging operations use to go about obtaining work for their crews and equipment. Both of these concerns, however, were beyond the scope of the present study. The focus here, instead, was on the job hunters and workers themselves.

Although the questions dealt with in this chapter were inspired quite directly by Granovetter's work, the focus is somewhat different. While Granovetter was concerned with the nature of the relationships which provided job information networks, he did not focus particularly on the geographic range of the networks. The range of job information networks is of central concern to the present study, because it relates to the logger's ability to adapt to shifts of supply and/or markets for logs.

Another important difference between this and Granovetter's study is that his white collar urban sample could hardly be described as an occupational community. Quite to the contrary, the major point of his book is that white collar jobs are usually obtained through linkages that result from relatively impersonal relationships. The expectation with which the present study was entered was that the set of network linkages which define the loggers occupational community serve also as channels through which information is conveyed concerning the availability of logging jobs.

Thus it was anticipated that two components of the logger's life, the labor market and community ties, would be highly interrelated and interdependent. This would present a sharp contrast to the experience of most Americans since the second half of the nineteenth century, as described by Bender (1978):

One's role as a member of a family or a circle of friends became sharply differentiated from one's role and behavior in economic relations, in dealing with the government, or in relations with any large-scale organizations. Within the first sphere, communal patterns of behavior, with their emphasis on face-to-face relationships, effective bonds, and diffuseness of obligation, remained appropriate and functional, but people painfully learned that these communal ways did not work in the larger society where their public activities were undertaken. (Bender, 1978: 117)

In this sense it was expected that loggers' networks would more closely resemble those of the English working class families described by Bott (1957):

In brief, connectedness does depend, in part, on the husband's occupation. If he is engaged in an occupation in which his colleagues are also his neighbors, his network will tend to be localized and its connectedness will tend to be high. If he is engaged in an occupation in which his colleagues are not his neighbors, his network will tend to become loose knit. (Bott, 1957: 105-106)

Prior to these studies there was little literature concerning Northwestern loggers that speaks directly to this question. However, an article by Colfer and Colfer (1978) that describes the differing social organization and lifestyles of public sector workers (mostly U.S. Forest Service employees and their families) and locals (mostly loggers and their families) who are residents of a logging town in western Washington addressed the issue tangentially. The authors described the public sector employees as "universalists" whose horizons, interests and personal contacts extend far beyond the local community. These are in contrast to the locals, to whom the authors assign the adjective "particularistic":

The approach [of the public employee] to life is universalistic, as is the bureaucratic mode of recruitment. Public employees like activities to be organized and efficient; they are frugal and interested in acquiring the material symbols of the middle class; they believe in going by the book, respecting authority, and following the rules; and they respect education.

The local way of life contrasts with this pattern. The number of local families is impossible to determine in the simple manner of public employees since place of employment if far from constant.

Likewise, kin ties extending into the neighboring hamlets and mobility among the hamlets blur the boundaries . . .

Although many local families have relatives in other cities and other parts of the country, most are heavily embedded in local kin networks. Kin ties, again maintained and nurtured by women, are called into play for economic cooperation, child care, assistance in time of need and for recreation. Where Forest Service families rely on bureaucratic ties for such services, locals turn to their kin. The isolation of the area and the lack of services encourage cooperation among people (Colfer and Colfer, 1978: 209-210).

It is unfortunate from the point of view of the present work that the Colfers did not focus more specifically on the role that the kin networks they describe play in conveying labor market information. It seems likely that at least a portion of these linkages cut across family lines and extend across fairly large geographic range, and thus fall into the category Bender (1978) calls community networks.

The set of expectations or tentative model, adopted at the beginning of the fieldwork and relating to the intersection of the logger's labor market and community ties, can be described as follows: First, it was anticipated that loggers would find jobs most frequently through the use of interpersonal network linkages rather than through formal job search and application procedures. It stands to reason that if Granovetter's urban, well-educated, white collar workers used informal means to find jobs, that loggers would be at least as likely to use interpersonal contacts in locating employment. Secondly, it was expected that the interpersonal networks used to obtain employment information would overlap with networks relating to the individual's personal and family life. In a more theoretical light, this prediction was seen as a potential indication of the lack of a clearly defined boundary between the occupational community member's work and off-duty life. Finally, it was expected that the loggers community/job networks would extend far beyond the boundaries of the geographic/political community in which he happened to reside at a particular time. This third component deserves some additional explanation.

The third component was inspired by the notion discussed in earlier chapters concerning non-geographic communities. This conception seemed to fit the logger due to the historically mobile nature of the industry. It was thought that the need for a logger to follow work would induce him and his family to develop a network of social attachment to others in the same situation, perhaps even to the exclusion of non-occupation members who happen to live in the same geographic location at any particular time. This was clearly the case for the turn of the century logging camp dweller. It was anticipated that the tradition of mobility in the industry and occupation would be carried on in the case of modern woods workers. It was expected at the outset that set of relatively highly developed job information networks would extend perhaps hundreds of miles up and down the West Coast, thus allowing loggers to readily adapt to geographic shifts in the availability of work. As will be seen below, this component of the "model" required significant alteration in light of the observations made in the fieldwork. Before the results with respect to this point are discussed, it will be useful to review what was found concerning other aspects of the model. We will begin with a discussion of job mobility in the occupation.

One of the traditions of logging that can be traced to the days of the logging camp is that of relatively short tenures for individuals with particular firms. Labor turnover was an accepted part of the life for logging operators. Individuals would work for as many as a half dozen operations in a given logging season. It is commonly said that an old-time logger would quit a job for no more reason than he ran out of "chew" and wanted to go to town to buy a new can. One retired logging superintendent for a large company was probably exaggerating only slightly when he stated that he used to have three crews: One on the way to the job, one working, and one coming back. The old-time loggers were noted for their lack of concern for job security. If an individual worked well when he was on the payroll, there were usually no hard feelings when he announced his departure. If an opening existed at another time, he would be welcomed back.

One retired old-time gyppo operator who was interviewed stated that, although he had a relatively stable crew consisting mostly of "locals," he would hire a few "tramp loggers" every season. These individuals, who were usually highly skilled and respected, would travel from place to place. They typically would make a circuit each year, staying just a few weeks to work in any given location. They were welcomed back each year because they were good workers. Although tramp logging survived for a period after the demise of the logging camp, older loggers stated that it, too, died out for the most part in the 1950s.

The passing of the old-time tramp logger and the logging camp did not, however, end the tradition of job mobility in the occupation. Although modern company loggers tend to remain with a firm for long periods of time, gyppo employees take pride in their freedom to change employers. In many cases, job changes among gyppo employees are motivated by little more than a slight pay increase, or a whim or a desire for a change in scenery or co-workers. One gyppo faller in his late 50s stated that he had never remained with a particular employer for more than four or five years. He said that he began to feel "trapped" or "fenced in" if he stayed on a job for too long. In other cases, job changing is a necessity. Gyppo operations, in particular, often expand and contract in size from year to year, sometimes leaving former employees without a job.

It became clear, during the earliest stages of the field research, that what at first appeared to be lack of concern for job security, particularly among gyppo loggers, was in fact confidence on the part of most that, under normal circumstances, another job can be obtained if the need arises. The individual derives his sense of job security (and, as we have seen above, also an important component of his sense of self) not from a necessarily long standing relationship with a particular firm, but rather from his marketability based on his reputation as a competent logger. There is a truism, which was repeated to the author dozens of times in the course of the initial fieldwork, that a good logger could, except in times of severe unemployment, almost always find work during the season.

The expectation that loggers would use informal means, as opposed to formal procedures, in finding work was borne out by the fieldwork. There is virtually no system of formal credentials in the logger's world. Loggers do not usually develop resumes, nor are they required (with the exception of truck drivers who are licensed by the states) to pass formal certification procedures. A high school diploma has not been a traditional requirement to a get a job in the woods. A portion of the loggers interviewed in both studies have some college education, but such education is not always seen as an asset with respect to one's ability to function in the occupation. The "certification" that carries the most weight in the logger's day to day world is one's reputation as someone who can play a productive role in getting the logs to town. Although some companies in the study areas did require prospective workers to file an application form at the company headquarters, interviewees indicated that most hiring decisions tended to be based on informal relationships and personal reputations in a way not dissimilar to how such decisions were made by gyppo operators.

There are essentially four ways that a prospective worker can go about obtaining employment in the woods or for a log trucking firm. The easiest of these is to return to work for an employer for whom one has previously worked. An individual who has successfully worked on a crew or driven a truck in the past for a particular employer is likely to have an advantage over someone without such direct experience. It is customary for logging operators to give the last year's crew members first chance at available jobs when logging "starts up" each spring. This custom is more formalized in the case of unionized companies who are often required to call individuals back to work in order of their seniority.

Another means of getting a job is to be known personally by the operator, siderod, or someone on the crew. In many cases, an existing crew member has worked with the individual for another employer. In others, the connection may simply be friendship or an acquaintanceship. During the participant-observation stage of the research a situation was noted in which a gyppo operator decided to hire an additional choker setter halfway through the logging season. One of the choker setters on the crew recommended a friend from his high school days. The choker setter was instructed to offer the individual the job, and the offer was accepted. The new choker setter did not meet his employer until he had been working with the crew for a number of days.

Kinship ties also often play a role in getting a logging job. Blood relatives, particularly children of owners of operations, are very often employed on crews and in many cases function in positions of responsibility that they might not otherwise have. For example, the siderod of the crew for whom the author was employed was the brother-in-law of the owner and the loader operator was the owner's son. (Note: At least two-thirds of the gyppo crews that the author encountered during the fieldwork had two or more individuals associated with them who were related by blood or marriage.) One pair of falling partners was encountered in which the younger man was divorced from the older man's daughter. In some cases, although no family ties exist between co-workers, the relationships have many of the characteristics of family relationships. One good example of this was the case of an older faller and two of his buckers whom he treated as sons. The relationship had many of the attributes of a family, including off-work time spent hunting and fishing together and occasional intense arguments so characteristic of many families.

In many cases, a well-respected logger can obtain employment for his son(s) on his or even another crew, by virtue of his own reputation. In some instances, a rigging slinger, catskinner or faller will persuade an operator to hire his son to work "behind" him to learn the ropes. The typical reasoning is that ". . . if old Joe is such a good logger, his boy probably has it in his blood." The new individual ultimately has to prove himself, but having a father in the business certainly provides an initial advantage.

An individual's reputation as a worker will usually play a crucial role in his getting work in the absence of any prior acquaintanceship with someone on the crew. In many cases a individual's reputation as a "fast" choker setter or a "high balling" cat skinner or truck driver will precede him. In some instances, work of his skill level may be passed along sequentially by several individuals before it reaches the potential employer. The author's observation is that, due in part to the absence of much formal certification in the logger's world, the single most important factor in an individual's obtaining work (provided, of course, that job opportunities exist at a given time) is his reputation. Individuals with well-established reputations in a particular area are usually the first to be offered work and (assuming they live up to their reputations) the last to be laid off.

When questioned about how they went about finding a new job, many experienced loggers replied they did not usually have to find work because "the job found them". They explained that if they put the "word" out among a few friends during the course of the off-season that they were seeking a new job, they would receive a call from prospective employers in the early spring. One experienced rigging slinger on a yarder side described an incident in which he became "fed up" with a particular job, quit in the middle of the day and began walking back toward town. He was picked up on the road and hired on the spot by the owner of another yarder operation who knew him by reputation and happened to be driving by.

It is difficult to overestimate the importance of an individual's work reputation for his success in finding a logging job, particularly in times of low demand. Employers and siderods described boom times when labor was scarce and they would try anyone ". . . who came in the door who looked like he could set a choker." However, under the economic circumstances which prevailed during the studies, employers could afford to be selective about whom they hired. As a result, individual workers tended to be very protective of their reputations. It is considered less of an offense to punch a logger in the nose than it is to unfairly sully his reputation as a worker. When discussing reputations and networks, a number of informants volunteered the view that information concerning bad reputations or "major screw ups" travels farther and faster than positive information about an individual or his accomplishments. There was universal agreement, however, that a worker's reputation is of the utmost importance to his success in obtaining a desirable job.

It is possible for an individual to be hired without prior references or network connections if an employer happens to be in immediate need. To carry this off, the applicant would be required to show up at the right place at the right time and emit the correct verbal, visual, and behavioral cues which would identify him as a logger, both during his initial encounter with the prospective employer and during his first days on the job. If he was making claim to rigging crew experience for example, he would be expected to know common logging terminology and general rigging crew procedures. The prospective employer would make initial judgments based on the way the applicant dressed, his size and physical stature, his speech patterns, and whether or not his demeanor seemed to indicate a willingness and ability to work hard. Once hired, the previously unknown worker would be required to demonstrate his skill during the first day or two on the job or face immediate dismissal. Employers are particularly wary about hiring an unknown individual to operate expensive equipment or to drive a truck.

The interviewees indicated that who calls whom in the process of a job search is not as important as one might predict. In some cases, the employer hears of the availability of an individual through a third party, in other cases the individual calls or contacts the employer or siderod directly. The crucial matter is the impression the employer has of the applicant and this is usually a matter of information he has gleaned through the network. Timing is, of course, also of central importance. In the case of an operator needing one additional hand to fill out an already working crew or one scheduled to begin, an individual's availability on a given day can be the deciding factor in his landing a job. In most cases, the crew is lined up in the late winter or early spring, weeks before an operation begins for the year.

As was hinted above, the geographic range of the loggers' job/community networks was found to be, in general, much more restricted than was originally anticipated. Loggers who work with or drive a truck for operations that utilize what we will label conventional technology (i.e., cats and conventional yarders) generally reported that they have a set of well developed job networks that cover a geographic area with a radius of approximately one hundred to one hundred and fifty miles. They also reported (not unexpectedly) that the density of their networks (i.e., the number of contacts) was higher closer to home and lower toward the outer range. Although the case study research design did not allow for any definitive testing on the matter, the investigation did uncover some evidence that indicated loggers' job networks for a given area tend to be geographically bound or segmented. Thus, for example, most loggers in community "X" tend to have about the same geographic distribution of networks that extend from the "Y" mountains to the "Z" river, and loggers on the other side of the mountain tend to have contacts that cover a discrete area on their side. It would thus be considerably more difficult for a logger from community "X" to find work on the other side of the mountain than it would for someone with well-established networks there. This subject deserves further research attention in the "post-owl" era.

It should be noted that the geographic ranges of networks described above should be regarded as tendencies rather than hard and fast rules. There were individuals encountered in the study who had previous experience in other areas or who had a limited number of job contacts in other places. It is increasingly common for northwestern loggers to find work in Alaska when none is available in the local area. Loggers who do travel to Alaska tend to do so only on a seasonal basis and to return home each winter. It was commonly said that life in an Alaskan logging camp is boring and tiresome.

The relatively small range of the loggers' networks was not anticipated at the outset of the initial fieldwork. In conjunction with this finding, the investigation uncovered unexpectedly strong ties on the part of loggers and their families to local areas. Loggers from all four categories tend to have strong ties to local areas and a localistic orientation. Many live within a few miles of their birthplace. Others have moved their families long distances once or twice in their careers but none interviewed has the mobile, rootless lifestyle, and social organization which characterized his turn of the century forebears. It appears, in short, that Holbrook and Hayner's "lumberjack" has indeed been tamed in this sense.

The relatively strong ties to local geographic areas are related to their families' local community relationships. Most loggers over the age of twenty-five are married and many have children in local schools. Their spouses and children tend to be well integrated into the local community. No evidence was uncovered for any particular propensity on the part of loggers' families to associate exclusively with the families of other loggers.

The loggers' geographic ties lead them to attempt to locate work within a reasonable distance of home. Most prefer to live at home and commute daily in operator provided transportation. As a general rule, if the commute is longer than an hour and a half to two hours each way, most choose to camp out on or near the job and commute on weekends. In some places, ownership of camp trailers has become as much a part of the logger's lifestyle as wearing hickory shirts or caulk boots.

The fieldwork uncovered some evidence that technology has an effect on the range of job networks and ties to local community. In one case, in the initial study area, the members of a crew of Swiss and Austrian born loggers led by a man who owns some specialized European long line yarding equipment were interviewed. His equipment is capable of spanning drainages a mile across and of yarding logs down as well as uphill. Although he had restricted his logging during the eight or so years prior to the interviews to the local area, he had worked previously in a number of locations extending from Central Washington through Northern California. His crewmen had potential job contacts in these areas by virtue of the fact that they had worked there with him. Unlike nearly all of the other individuals interviewed for the study, the members of this crew professed to have no ties to any particular geographic area. They are reminiscent of the old-time tramp loggers in that they claim to be happy to go wherever the demand for their work takes them. The effects of their European backgrounds and psychological ties to their communities of birth in Europe were impossible to sort out from the effects of technology in attempting to explain their lack of strong ties to any geographic area in the United States.

The other example of the effect of technology on the range of job networks is the case of helicopter loggers. Helicopter operations typically cover a multi-state area in any given year, and their crews usually spend at least half of the year away from home. Helicopter loggers develop job networks that correspond to the range of their work. Helicopter crew members stated that they continue to have ties to their home communities, but that their relationships to friends and neighbors in the home community have been weakened by the amount of time they are required to spend away from home. If the helicopter logging continues to grow as an economically viable technology (which appears quite likely given increasing concern about disturbance of more sensitive sites by ground based technology), it appears that helicopter rigging crews will continue to evolve into a specialized group of workers with a working world distinct from that of other loggers. It is difficult to conceive of such a mobile group of individuals maintaining strong local ties.

Conclusion

The initial expectation that logging jobs would be obtained through the use of informal networks rather than formal job search procedure was clearly borne out in the fieldwork. The major difference between the findings reported here and those of Granovetter is that the job networks he reports tended to be based on impersonal "loose" ties as opposed to the more dense community ties that were found among loggers. This could be taken as further evidence, if any were needed, that loggers constitute an occupational community. We have reported the importance of the individual's reputation as a worker to his obtaining employment due at least in part to the absence of any formal certification procedure in the industry.

Although the expectation that loggers' networks would extend beyond the boundaries of geographic community was substantiated, the geographic range of his networks was found, in the study areas examined to be unexpectedly small. This finding was related to the relatively strong ties to local areas that loggers and their families exhibited. These findings have some important implications with respect to the logger's ability to adapt to geographic shifts in the availability of harvestable timber or markets for logs. The logger's strong affective ties to local areas and the geographic limitations of his job finding/community networks tend to be mutually reinforcing. He likes a particular area, so he develops social and work ties there and this, in turn, tends to reinforce his liking of the area.

This set of arrangements works to his advantage until a major problem develops relative to either supply of or demand for timber. If either supply or demand dries up in an area, the logger (particularly the woods logger as opposed to the road builder or trucker) faces a very difficult set of circumstances. He typically has few, if any, other realistic employment options in his local area and could face a difficult period of reintegration in another area, assuming he could find an area where wood products employment was available.

7

The Logger and the Spotted Owl

Fighting over the control and disposition of land and natural resources in the American West is a tradition at least as old as European settlement of the region. The outcomes of such conflicts have had important consequences, not only for the land and natural resources in question, but also for the stakeholders in the battles. One need only contrast the wealth accumulated by some early development interests with the fate suffered by most native peoples in the nineteenth century to be reminded of how severe can be the consequences of winning or losing the struggle for access to the land upon which one's prosperity and/or way of life depends (Limerick, 1987).

The purpose of this chapter is to discuss some of the consequences which have unfolded as a result of owl/old-growth struggle. The specific consequences of focus are those for loggers in the communities studied with some comparison provided concerning consequences for other residents of the logging towns in which the fieldwork was conducted.

During the summer of 1990 as he passed through Seattle on the way to one of the field sites for this study, the author observed a billboard with the message: "OWLS vs. JOBS" on a Metro bus in Seattle. The sign went on (in much smaller print) to advertise a television news program " . . . reports at 6 and 11: 00." Nearly anyone who was involved in the spotted owl controversy could find something objectionable in that often repeated characterization of the dispute. It ignored, for example, the more general habitat and ecological dimensions, as well as the temporal and philosophical underpinnings of the issue. The "Owls vs. Jobs" characterization also greatly oversimplified the social impacts resulting from the controversy itself and from the abrupt changes in allocations of public timber, as we will note below. It also, of course, ignored the broader context of the issue and the other pressures playing on loggers and their communities as we discussed in Chapter 3. The present chapter can be seen as an attempt to move beyond the billboard/sound bite portrayal that worker/community dimension of the the issue has so often received.

During the same summer, the spotted owl controversy became the subject of considerable attention in the national media and at high levels in the federal government. One report (in a syndicated radio newscast), quoted a sub-cabinet official in the executive branch as stating that the potential job losses resulting from increased timber harvest restrictions were not particularly significant because " . . . [a]nyone can find another job; people do it all the time." Statements such as that, reflecting a highly rationalistic labor market conception of human behavior, were encountered frequently in the media as the controversy generated more attention. Another common expression of this view was the argument that Northwestern forest products workers are simply part of the regional economy of the Northwest, and that they would adjust "one way or the other".

The labor market perspective may well be a valid characterization of the relationships of workers to jobs inside the Beltway, or in the Silicon Valley. However, in view of the knowledge gained in the first study, there are serious questions to be asked about the adequacy of that model to account for the behavior of loggers. It fails to account for important dimensions of the circumstances of loggers and other forest products workers suddenly displaced and facing the prospect of no future employment in their occupation, or perhaps in any rural setting at all.

There is no question that people do "adapt" to exogenous economic and political forces over which they have little or no control. However, the significant issues of concern in this case revolve around the nature of those adaptations and the social costs likely to be incurred. In short, the labor market view appears simplistic, seeming to ignore culture, identity, the social meaning attached to particular kinds of work, and the mediating effects that these forces might exert on behavior in times of change and stress. The impact study was undertaken to examine the potential local impacts of the unfolding controversy by means of indepth personal interviews with, and firsthand observations of, a portion of those who stood to be affected. A key objective was to identify and document from a very empirical standpoint, the key influences and social processes important for understanding the community impacts of the controversy as they were beginning to emerge.

It is important to note that the timing of the study required that the interviews and observations be conducted at a time when the final outcome of the issue was far from clear. Thus, what is presented here is a portrayal of the impacts of a controversy in progress rather than an *ex post facto* portrait. As will be seen, the results suggest that these impacts can be understood at least partially in light of patterns remarkably consistent with those described in the work of Hayner, Holbrook, and the first study we have discussed in previous chapters of this volume. In light of their historical persistence, it seems unlikely that these patterns of identity formation and reinforcement, in-group socialization, reputation building and the like will disappear completely as a consequence of the owl/old-growth issue. This question will be revisited following the presentation of the results of the impact study below.

The interviews conducted in 1990 revealed patterns of occupational community dynamics among western Washington loggers strikingly parallel to those identified in the prior fieldwork. The following comment by one such logger captured a very familiar sentiment:

> Most all my friends are loggers. I have a lot of respect for other loggers because I know what they do. It comes out of really knowing the hard work and the danger that they face. Besides, a logger is someone you can really count on anytime, for anything.

Insights also came from logger's spouses. One described her husband as follows:

> He was born a logger. That's just who he is. His grandfather was a timber cutter. He loves it. I can tell you that no matter what happens, he's gonna be in the woods . . . period.

Another interviewee (in his twenties) related that when he graduated from high school, his mother presented him with a new set of rigging cloths and a pair of caulk boots and his father gave him a ticket to Juneau, Alaska, so he could more readily "break in" as a faller. He subsequently worked several summers as a faller in Alaska and "on the rigging" in Washington during the winters until he was able to find a job as a faller in Washington. He acknowledged that, in light of the owl controversy, the future of logging is uncertain in his area but stated that he wanted to "stay and fight" and, if necessary, be "the last one in [his community] to turn out the lights."

An interview with a young hook tender early in the fieldwork uncovered another variation on this theme that was to resurface throughout the study. The discussion turned at one point to the future of logging, and the interviewee went on at considerable length concerning the reasons why there was "no future" in the business. He stated that he could forsee a time in the not too distant future when there would be no logging. At a later point in the interview when he was queried about his own plans, he stated that he planned to "tend hook" for about fifteen years and then "get up on a piece of equipment" to finish out his career.

When asked what he would do if no logging jobs were available, he responded that he would "get cedar". When asked what would happen if no woods work were available, he had a difficult time answering. Finally he stated that he might have to get a job in the mill.

It became increasingly clear in the course of this exchange that he was approaching the future of his occupation on two different levels. At the intellectual level he clearly recognized the problematic future of logging. However, he approached the issue very differently on a personal level, apparently because logging was all he had ever imagined in his personal future. This was a common pattern among loggers interviewed and was frequently commented on by spouses of loggers.

Even those who leave logging have regrets, such as those expressed by a former logger who had, several years prior to the controversy, taken a job for the local telephone company. In the following excerpt from fieldnotes of an interview, this logger describes the influence of the occupational identity on his life:

_____ had made a deliberate effort to leave the logging occupation, but he stated that he misses it and . . . has never had a job so satisfying as working in the woods. He said that if the certainty and benefits were better in the woods, despite the fact that he is now over 40, he would go back in a minute, because he loved the work so much. He misses it a great deal. He talked about how he had the privilege to work with some of the highest production logging outfits in the western United States, and how proud that made him feel. He said that pushing until one's limits are reached is a tremendously satisfying experience, and one that he will value forever. He looks back on the period when he did some of the things he did in the woods and realizes he could never do that again, and that it's a kind of a dream, but . . . a very important part of who he is.

In comparison to the earlier fieldwork, there was evidence of a heightened self-consciousness in workers' (and in some instances their families') identification with the occupation and associated way of life. This, in apparent response to the crisis, was reflected in respondents' particular eagerness to bring up in conversations and interviews both the importance of wood products to the economy (and especially to the urban economy) and the unique features and special knowledge involved in a logging/rural way of life. Signs were posted in yards and businesses proclaiming "This family [business] supported by timber dollars." While some of this might be dismissed as political rhetoric, the tone of interviews reflected genuine surprise at the lack of understanding by many outsiders concerning the way of life in the occupation, and in occupation-linked, communities and the potential local consequences of the issue. This lack of understanding led to an impulse to articulate to others (and, in effect, to themselves) the meaning and value of that which was threatened. Quoting again from fieldnotes:

> _____ is quite aware of the "urban view" of the timber issue and of logging, and he says that he is pretty negative about that view. He feels that rural America's values are very important -- hard work and hanging together -- and that those values are possibly disappearing, and that the country will be poorer for it.
> [He said] that although fewer people . . . actually work in the timber industry in _____, the ethic of the industry and of logging influences the entire community, and that people who live here, even though they do not necessarily work in the industry, are very much affected by the hard work, hard play, helping each other kind of ethic that comes from logging. He finds it interesting that some of the most radical people relative to the political developments in the area are merchants who have moved into the area within the last 10 years. Another trend that he described is the increased presence of government workers in recent years in the area, including school teachers, Forest Service employees, prison guards, etc. He feels, however, that the culture is still very much dominated by the logging ethos. He also stated that if the perception of being disenfranchised continues, and if the developments continue in a very negative way relative to the viability of the local way of life, he is concerned about the potential for violence on the part of some members of the community.

This pattern of increased self consciousness about one's way of life in time of externally locused threat is comparable to that described by Gold (1985) in the case of western ranching communities threatened by the changes resulting from the arrival of mineral development interests. The intrusions led ranchers to reemphasize the tradition of "neighboring," which was a long standing element of ranching culture:

> In general, most ranchers felt that a demented value system was being imposed on them, that their Western hospitality and trust were being violated, and that they like their land were considered expendable. These feelings came from the . . . struggle between . . . the economically and politically powerful interventionists and . . . the economically and politically reactive locals.
> Commenting on the fragility of the situation, one informant stated: "That sums it all up. . . . We need each other to survive. Until this coal business entered our lives, we had been acting as though we were good neighbors but we had actually been drifting apart. Now we have to really be good neighbors again or we are going to be easy pickings for the industrialists" (Gold 1985: 56).

Another pervasive theme in the interviews of the current study was that of the stress the timber crisis was causing for workers, spouses and families:

> _____ made the point that the community . . . cannot stand the strain of not knowing its future. He said that "absolutely the worst part of the whole thing" was the uncertainty; that he cannot make plans or buy anything, because he just doesn't know what his job will be tomorrow. He thought that the people making policy do not really care what happens to the average worker. He stated that " . . . if they figure that in six months, things will stabilize, well, six months would be too long for the average worker in _____ to go without working."

In addition to the stress of "not knowing" about the future of jobs, the owl/old-growth controversy (along with other constraints on timber availability) created other problems. Contractors and companies began to bid on sales farther away from "home". This change, and related circumstances, created further stress. As a logger's spouse stated:

> _____ spoke about how she felt that women in the community bear most of the stress that happens to the family. She explained at length how the loggers [now] often have to go away to log for weeks at a time. They're away for longer and longer periods of time, and . . . the women have to run the entire household. They have to do all the economic work of the household: paying all the bills, etc., in addition to doing all the housework and making all the decisions about raising the children and disciplining them. The wives also take care of the outside of the house, mow the lawn, and so on. This is really difficult even for a housewife, and especially difficult for a working wife of a logger. It puts a lot of stress on the women. Concurrently, women are worrying about the health of their husbands, because logging is such a dangerous occupation.

The same interview went on:

> Finally, _____ spoke about how she felt that women were [often] the sole emotional support for most of the men . . . [who] often don't speak to each other about any of their worries or fears, and that often their wives [are] the only people [with whom]husbands share [such worries]. In addition to the stress the woman is bearing in terms of [her responsibilities], she . . . has to be the sole emotional support, and . . . "be there" for her husband whenever he needs her. Often that is too much, and . . . some women just cannot bear that stress, . . . and the resulting overload leads to . . . difficulties such as alcoholism, marital problems, family problems, and sometimes even abuse within the family. She also spoke about how women will turn to each other and

look to each other for help in bearing all of their burdens. She . . . mentioned the church as a place she felt she could go in order to get help, but she [estimated] that only about [half] of the community would be comfortable going to the church for help.

Another interviewee (also the spouse of a logger) described how the owl issue was adding to the difficulties she and her husband had experienced as a result of the economic downturn in the 1980s:

They worked for many years as an independent logging firm until 1984, when due to market fluctuations, the firm they were contracting for filed Chapter 11. They were owed $184,000.00 and had two years of logging contracts signed in advance. They had $80,000.00 invested in their home, and in two more years it would have been paid for. They had had their own logging firm for eighteen years at this point. As the months went by and they weren't paid back, and the court process dragged on, they ended up losing their home and being evicted. During this time, _____'s husband took several contracting jobs with logging firms and did some construction work. Meanwhile, _____ did some nursing, and was eventually hired by _____.

_____ said she had a very hard time dealing with the loss of her business, and though she had friends that she could talk to and help her deal with the situation, her husband really had trouble. There weren't many people he could talk to or turn to for help. At the same time, because of what had happened to them and the hard times they were facing, it was even more difficult for either of them to gain employment and to look for work, because the whole town knew what had happened to them and knew that they were having a hard time.

Accompanying the strong identification and the stress the issue was placing on workers and families, the interviews revealed a ground swell of anger at those whom loggers viewed as threatening their way of life. One observer noted that most loggers had, until recently, spent their lives believing that if they worked hard, their families would be provided for. Now it seemed that the rules had changed with little notice and potentially disastrous consequences. Another interviewee addressed the same theme:

I worry about my kids. What are they learning from this? I have always taught them to work hard and be honest, yet now they see me suffering despite the fact that I have worked hard my whole life. It has to make them cynical to watch what is happening to me.

Much of the frustration and anger was aimed at environmentalists who, from the local perspective, have little at stake in terms of their day to day lives in the decisions they influence:

_____ was upset by the idea that outsiders were being misled about the lifestyle and the realities of living in a timber community. She felt particularly insulted by the degrading comments about logging and the misconception that people who live in logging communities are not concerned with the environment. She also felt that logging was a serious commitment (she related how her sister-in-law had two brothers killed in the woods), so that it was particularly distressing to hear people talk down about logging, or to make a joke out of it, and hear people talk about "stupid loggers," etc. She wanted to see a lot more education about the timber industry, and in particularly, logging. She also wanted to see more education about the forest and the renewable nature of the forest, because she felt that outsiders, who weren't accustomed to being around the forest were so easily [misled] by the press and other interest groups.

One interviewee, discussing dealings with environmentalists, stated wryly that "compromise is defeat on the installment plan." Others focused more generally on those with urban interests, who were seen as misinformed about the forest and ignorant of, or coldly indifferent to, the consequences for timber workers of the dramatic reductions being proposed in timber harvesting rates:

I've lived and worked in the woods all my life; I love it. If I didn't love it, I wouldn't be here. . . . I depend on the woods. How can anyone who knows less than I do about the woods say that I am not an environmentalist?

A very persistent theme in the interviews and observations was that the spotted owl controversy was widely perceived in the communities studied as fundamentally a clash of urban versus traditional rural cultures with the latter is being overwhelmed and devalued by the former. The owl was seen as a stalking horse, furthering the interests of environmental groups at the expense of people whose lives and livelihoods depend on harvesting and processing trees. This led, for many, to a profound sense of betrayal. When interviewed one logger stated: "We feel attacked . . . For us the American dream is being betrayed."

Those sentiments were shared in varying degrees of intensity by most community groups encountered in the 1990 to 1991 impact studies. With some exceptions (which will be discussed below), community residents generally expressed the view that their lives and livelihoods were hanging in the balance of decisions being influenced by, and ultimately made by, urban-based interests and decision makers who have little knowledge or interest in how those decisions would affect the local way of life. The "urban versus rural" values and perceptions theme emerged in interview after interview. "It's as if working people are being punished. The government and the media are siding with people who aren't honest or hard working. . . they are siding with rich people who don't get their hands dirty."

Another interviewee echoed a similar theme:

> _____ is very concerned with how the public is viewing loggers and logging communities, and she spoke at length about this. She's concerned that people from the outside don't understand what goes on in the logging towns, and they don't see this personal side or the personal tragedy should there be an end to, or a cutback in, the timber industry.

It is useful to recall that a similar theme was evident in research conducted in California by Fortmann and Kusel (1990) and more recently in interviews conducted with poor and working-class women by Beverly Brown (1991) in an area in southwest Oregon that has been historically dependent on timber extraction. One important difference between both the Fortmann and Kusel and Brown studies and this case arises from the fact that the other author's study areas are inhabited by significant numbers of immigrants from urban areas (referred to as newcomers) with values quite different than those of most long-standing locals. This has resulted in internal community conflict:

> Several of my interview subjects complained about the comments popular among the newcomers . . . Casual jokes about how backward and reactionary the locals are can be heard in any crowd of non-locals. I heard a typical one just the other day when a friend said she just didn't want to go to a meeting where she had to "hear the yokels yammering away about jobs" (Brown, 1991: 13).

Brown also comments:

> If the Spotted Owl is seen as a symbol for gentrification, for the ability of urban-origin middle class newcomers to unilaterally enforce their agendas, and in the process, cut off access of local people to homes and land, does local resistance become more intelligible? (Brown, 1991: 11).

Returning to the western Washington study, many loggers interviewed expressed a profound sense of disillusionment that their country could allow "such a thing" to happen to them. One informed the interviewers that he was thinking of leaving the U.S.:

> "If this thing happens [the listing], I might just move out of this country . . . Just because I feel so disgusted and betrayed by the government."

Another issue that emerged was frustration and anger at how the issue was frequently presented in the (urban) press, and particularly how the role of the logger and the way of life in the communities were portrayed:

> [He] said that he felt as though the media has treated people of ____ like "shit". He said that "they are depicting us as barbarians and idiots, and that we are raping the forest," and he said that he feels really angry at this depiction of his community . . . that it is completely false, and that he feels sorry for urbanites who are taken in by these falsehoods, because . . . they are "ignorant" and are "being misled." [He] again [stated] that the media was a big part of this, and told the story of how the media had misquoted him, and "made him look like an idiot" . . . He said that the [major urban newspaper] especially seemed to want to write stories that make the plight of timber towns look humorous, and he thought that they were all just treating the people out here like they were "one big joke".

One of the types of media portrayals that resulted in the most anger was that of editorial cartoons that depicted a (typically overweight, unintelligent appearing) logger cutting the last tree in sight, apparently unconcerned about the environmental consequences and blissfully unaware that he is destroying his own livelihood. This portrayal was seen by interviewees as dishonest and offensive for several reasons. One was the logger's purported lack of both intelligence and concern for the sustainability of the forest:

> _____ said that he got angry when people he'd meet outside of the area would express stereotypes about loggers and say that loggers were dirty, stupid people. Often when he would tell people that he was a logger, at school or wherever, they would be surprised and say that they thought loggers were not as smart as he was, or just express other stereotypes about loggers. He also said that when he was younger he might have said that you should clear-cut America, or to clear-cut, burn and pave America, and he felt like the minority of loggers who had ever expressed that opinion had been singled out in the media, or used as examples for all loggers. He felt that the majority of loggers were much

more environmentally conscious and much more concerned with the woods than the average person. It angered him that other people didn't see loggers this way.

Another media portrayal to which loggers objected was the notion that there were virtually no trees left to harvest. Most offensive, however, was the message that loggers, (that is *workers* as opposed to land owners, industry decision makers, and state and federal agencies) were responsible for past harvesting allocations and decisions and thus had created their own dilemma. Interviewees stated that after a spate of "negative coverage" the print and television media did run some stories giving the "other side" of the story. By this time the damage had been done, both in terms of influencing "outsider" perceptions and blaming of workers for a set of circumstances completely outside of their control.

A related issue in the interview data is a sense of disenfranchisement and powerlessness on the part of loggers (and many other locals) from the the administrative and judicial processes that set the course for forest land decision-making. At key points in the controversy, a complex array of administrative and judicial decisions were announced on a frequent (at times nearly weekly) basis. Interviewees reported a sense of frustration and emotional exhaustion from attempting to make sense of what was occurring and to interpret the short- and long-term consequences of each announcement. A common topic of conversation was the burden placed on them and their families by the uncertainty created by a complexity and consequently vague series of decision-making processes that were affecting their lives and livelihoods:

> The uncertainty and powerlessness is unbearable. I think about it all the time. Every day, hour minute I am worried about what will happen. Maybe my mind will wander away from it for a bit but it always comes back.
>
> The people living here are like condemned prisoners. They don't know the day or time of their execution. That uncertainty is hanging over our heads.

Once again, Brown describes similar themes from her Oregon study:

> In the minds of many environmental activists, the trees were being saved from the ignorant "rednecks" -- read: local working-class people -- who, it was assumed, were dupes of the transnational forest companies and captives of an outmoded frontier mentality (Brown,1991: 10).

None of this was lost on the loggers and most others interviewed for the Washington study. Whatever "labor market" adaptations eventually take place in response to decreases in timber-related employment, they seem likely to occur, for many in the study areas, within a context of anger and alienation. The logger's building frustration stems from increasingly complex, and even uncertain, political and administrative decision-making processes that are viewed as dominated by people who neither understand, nor particularly care about, the circumstances of loggers and their communities. Political alienation by woods workers and some others in logging communities may well prove to be to the longest term negative social impact of the forest controversy.

As the above discussion has hopefully communicated, an overarching theme (which emerged from the interviews and observations for the impact study) was the existence of tension and conflict between loggers and other locals on the one hand and the (mostly urban) interests on the other, as the latter continued to seek to protect old-growth forests from harvest. A less obvious, but nonetheless present, theme was tension between workers and the decision- makers in the forest industry. This was most obvious among sawmill workers and former sawmill workers in one study site, as they had lived through a strike against the largest mill in the area several years prior to the study. The strike was broken by the company. Workers who stayed out (many out of loyalty to their co-workers, rather than a personal preference for the strike) lost their jobs. These workers were then faced with a choice of moving from the community or long commutes to other places of industrial employment. Several had chosen employment with an oil refinery and opted for the commute. Others had left the community. Loggers in the area, all of whom were contractors or employed by contractors, had been mixed in their view of the labor dispute. Several reported having crossed the picket lines during the strike.

Another example of tension between workers and industry surfaced in discussions with both gyppo and company loggers, who stated that they believed that the large land holding forest products companies stood to gain from the crisis and might even be quietly in favor of increased logging restrictions on public lands. All were in agreement that it was the smaller operators and their employees who stood to lose the most in the crisis. Some even speculated that large land-owning timber companies might be directly complicit with environmentalists in fomenting the crisis. Many expressed a feeling of helplessness in the face of powerful forces on multiple sides of the issue, none of which seemed to be operating in their interests.

Another source of tension between workers and industry management emerged in interviews with women, who either were active, or chose not to be active, in a timber advocacy group sponsored in large part by industry. The following excerpt from fieldnotes provides insight into this tension and ambiguity:

> I spoke with her at length about the role of [the timber advocacy group]. I asked . . . why she wasn't more active in the organization . . . at first she said that she didn't really get along with the [group's] people . . . and that she had disagreements with . . . the way they presented things. She said she was afraid that [the group] was too negative, and that it didn't really deal with the issues that women were facing. Finally, later in the conversation, she said that she felt that [the group] was just [public relations] for the industry, and that was one of the main reasons she didn't feel that she should get involved. She felt that it was really important, especially during this crisis, to acknowledge the existence of three separate groups. One would be the environmentalists; two, the industry and its owners (for whom she feels [the group] speaks and does [public relations]) and the third group, made up of timber industry workers and their families. [She] pointed out that although the media tends to lump . . . workers and the industry together, those two groups, while they have some things in common, definitely have some differences. At the same time, [she] expressed fear around making these distinctions clear, because they could be interpreted as being anti-industry. In the current climate, it could be used against industry, and she feels very much tied to the industry . . . She certainly didn't want to give any ammunition to the environmentalists. At the same time, she felt that she didn't really trust [the company] . . . In her words: "They could turn around and lay my husband off tomorrow."

The loggers interviewed for this study clearly felt themselves to be under direct attack by environmentalists and overwhelmed politically by the urban majority. While tensions did exist with industry, these were far less obvious. The most apparent reason for this was the nature of the controversy itself in the sense that the immediate protection of old-growth previously slated for harvest would be result in dramatic job losses. The underlying issue, however, was cultural. Loggers and their families perceived far greater cultural distance between themselves and the environmental community than they felt between themselves and industry decision-makers. Thus, for the loggers interviewed for this study, the spotted owl dispute had become a battle in which a culture and way of life were under attack and at risk.

Other Community Stakeholder Groups

Before turning to a summary and conceptualization of impacts of the controversy on loggers and their families, it will be useful to briefly describe the circumstances of stakeholder groups other than loggers in the communities studied. Although loggers (as an occupational community) are the primary subject of this volume, a comparison of their circumstances to others in the communities will aid in understanding why it may be possible for the communities as a whole to weather the crisis, while certain groups within the communities may find adaptation far more problematic. These summary descriptions are in no sense indepth analyses and are intended only to provide a basis of comparison and additional context for the discussion of loggers and the crisis.

Community Business People

People in this category are, for the most part, proprietors or employees of small independent businesses, such as grocery, drug and hardware stores, restaurants, service stations, and the like. They tend to be very committed to small town life and often work very hard to promote the image and well being of the "town" as the center of the local lifestyle. Local business people tend to comprise the political leadership of communities and are usually at the core of any locally-based economic diversification efforts. Such people have often invested their life savings in one or more local enterprises, and their fortunes have tended (in the past, at least) to rise and fall with those of the timber industry in the immediate area.

It should be noted, however, that the interests of local business people are seen as somewhat different than those of timber workers. While some identify with the industry, others tend to value an environment of economic stability for their enterprises and thus are often in some tension with forest products people over the issue of economic diversification. Said one:

> As a community member, and especially as a business person, I am under a tremendous amount of pressure to "take sides," [in the Spotted Owl controversy] to commiserate for people here constantly about the situation. Don't get me wrong, I am concerned for them and for the community, but I think I am personally going to make it. My future is bright here in town regardless of downturns in the timber industry."

Sawmill Workers

Unlike logging, the nature of the work carried out by most employees in sawmills tends to be repetitive and very routinized. The ability to complete a specified task consistently and efficiently is valued over independence and creativity. The work environment tends to be closely controlled. Due, in part, to these circumstances, there has been, in recent generations, a much stronger tradition of unionization in the sawmills and more worker-management conflict than is generally found in the case of woods work (Robbins, 1989).

The interviews we conducted suggest that sawmill workers' occupational identities, and the importance placed on occupation as a life interest, tend to be quite different than is the case for loggers. To be sure, there are parallels in terms of pride in skill in the case of more highly skilled mill jobs such as sawyer or millwright, but the intense identification with one's particular work, which is the hallmark of membership in the loggers' occupational community, was not generally found among sawmill workers interviewed. Sawmill workers were observed to be as likely to identify with organized labor as with sawmill occupations per se. Many did, however, express concern and resentment at the possibility of being forced from their occupation with few viable options. Many said that they would be happy enough to take equivalent employment, if such were available in their community. Most did express serious reservations about the disruptive consequences for themselves and their families of being forced to relocate to an urban area. Most expressed a strong attachment to small town life, citing its advantages for raising children and its personalized atmosphere.

Shake and Shingle Workers

Another stakeholder group of relevance to this discussion is that comprised of people in the shake and shingle industry. These workers are typically employed in independent, often family-run mills, that process cedar in the manufacture of siding and roofing materials. Those interviewed for the impact study tended to express less commitment to their occupation than is the case for loggers, though they still expressed very strong attachment to their homes and family/friendship networks. Many stated that moving would be the "last thing" they would do if they lost their jobs, because at a stressful time such as that, their support network would be more important than ever.

_____ said that he has no idea what else he would do besides packing shingles, because he has done it his whole life. When I asked him what his options would be, if he could no longer pack shingles, and he said that he would never do anything else; that if he couldn't pack shingles anymore, that he would likely go on welfare, because he felt that it was too late in his life to retrain for anything else, and that he had no intention of moving.

Shake and shingle workers who find themselves unemployed are in somewhat different circumstances than other timber workers. On the one hand, a higher proportion of shake and shingle workers tend to be self employed than is the case for others in the industry; consequently they are not eligible for the usual unemployment benefits. On the other hand, shake and shingle mill employees can be eligible for Trade Adjustment assistance in light of their industry's status relative to competition with foreign trade. This program has a lengthy certification procedure, but it offers an extended period of cash benefits, as well as job search and (ironically perhaps) relocation assistance.

The following is from an interview with a small shake mill owner:

_____ is very attached to [his home town]. He doesn't want to lose his home, or move out of the area. He said that he would much rather get a new job, no matter what it is, as long as he didn't have to move and he could afford to keep his house . . .
[He]said that the stress is really difficult for him to face. He is afraid of having to sell his home and move. He said that the stress was so great on his relationship that his wife has recently left him and moved to North Dakota . . . [He] said that it's extremely stressful, because at 47 he doesn't know how to do anything else, and it's difficult for him to think about being retrained. He says that he's applied for 10 different jobs in the last 6 months and has been turned down for all of them, despite the fact that he's qualified for several different positions. He feels that because of his age, that he's not wanted by employers. Also, working in the shake mill has effected his health and made him a risk physically to hire and that also is preventing him from being hired in another occupation.

Women

As one might expect, the interviews revealed that women play a complex variety of roles in the communities in which the studies were conducted. These vary from head sawyer in a sawmill, shingle worker, and small business owner to book keeper, financial manager, mother, and spouse. No women were identified who were employed as loggers. Most of the women interviewed had jobs outside the home *and* primary responsibility for housekeeping, household financial management, and child care. Most cited financial need as the primary reason for working outside the home.

The complexity with respect to women, and which was revealed in the interviews, in the three study communities inspired additional data collection and analysis (Warren, 1992; Warren, Lee, and Carroll, 1992). One very clear pattern identified is a perception on the part of a variety of women that they absorb a significant proportion of the stress resulting from proposed harvest reductions. Expressed concerns centered around possible job losses and the resulting strain, both emotional and economic on their families. Specific reasons for this range from tension resulting from changes in long routinized activities and anticipation of having to move away from extended families to fears concerning their husband's ability to adapt to other kinds of work. Women also expressed concerns related to their own ability to hold up under stress, including family financial crises, demands for emotional support from husbands and children, and the possible breakdown of family coping mechanisms. This particular dimension of the crisis will be explored separately in future analyses.

Summary and Analysis

The results of this study suggest that the circumstances beginning to be faced by loggers and some other community residents in the two study sites suffering the direct effects of the owl issue have at least some characteristics in common with other situations described by sociologists and others as "human disasters" (Lee, Carroll, and Warren, 1991). There is considerable literature in sociology and psychology about the dimensions and consequences of disasters for human communities and groups. According to the work of Barton, a human disaster situation involves:

1. limiting or denying the realization of expectations,

2. as a result of identifiable causes,

3. which result in final cumulative and overwhelming stress on a community or group.

Such stress is the result of people failing to receive "expected conditions of life" such as "physical safety . . . provision of food, shelter and income and guidance and information necessary to carry on normal activities"(Barton, 1970: 38). The author goes on to say that such conditions can arise from causes internal (i.e., strikes or severe political disorganization) or external to a social system or community. Among the potential external causes noted are floods, droughts, earthquakes, loss of markets, or supply of important materials. The author goes on to state:

> It should be noted that a collective stress may be limited to a small system, or it may come to a small system in the context of a general stress on a much larger system of which it is a part (Barton, 1970: 39).

The following are additional exerpts from interview notes from the second logger's spouse described in the last chapter:

> _____ seems greatly concerned about what's going to happen to her community. She's afraid that her community will not be able to stand up under the stress of job displacement, and that individuals will not be able to cope with their loss of their occupation, since it is so closely tied in with their identity. She relates to her own experience, and how difficult it was for her and her husband, and what it did to their marriage. She feels that she's a strong person who is able to cope, and she barely made it. She's really concerned that there are many members of her community that will not make it through such a time.
> _____ wonders who people can turn to for help, especially when it comes to these domestic problems that will be increasing as pressure increases and stress increases on the community. In general, in spite of_____ 's identification of the cohesiveness and strength of the community, she's really concerned that the possible job loss is going to be too much for the individuals, and lead to a lot of problems involving alcohol, spousal abuse, and suicide. Currently, _____ felt that the members of the community hadn't fully realized what was happening to them, and that the worst was yet to come in terms of people accepting the fact, or dealing with the fact that there are going to be cutbacks in the timber industry.

The external conditions in the larger society which led to these circumstances, were long in the making. With the benefit of hindsight, it can be seen that the timber supply/land reclassification dilemma had been building for decades. As we noted in the previous chapter, the prolonged recession in the early 1980s had inflicted significant economic difficulties and uncertainties on forest products workers in the study areas. Many interviewees indicated that they and their families were still recovering from the effects of that period when the owl issue emerged. One of the traditions which had survived once again had to do with "riding out" the bad times and relying on one's reputation to generate employment opportunities in better ones. This strategy, as we have noted, leaves workers particularly vulnerable if the "good times" fail to return. It is also significant, as will be suggested below, that the circumstances described in this chapter were triggered in the end by political, rather than economic, developments.

Three points should be made in invoking the term "human disaster" in the present context. One is that the investigation uncovered the *potential* for human disaster, not its actual manifestation. Secondly, it seems unlikely that overall social and economic conditions in the *geographic* communities studied will approximate those described in Barton. Where the potential for at least some manifestation of human disaster seemed most apparent was for particular occupational groups linked to forest products. The third point is that because the negative consequences are likely to be distributed unevenly across groups in the geographic locales (or former locales, if displaced groups leave their homes in search of greener pastures) they may be less visible. Much has been written about the "invisibility" of rural poverty (Fitchen, 1991; Humphrey et al., 1993)

The owl/forest controversy resulted in two separate, but related, consequences for many loggers and their families:

1. threatened loss of jobs and
2. degradation of identities and culture.

At the time of the study, the latter effect was already strongly felt, while the former was, for the most part, still at the anticipation stage. The latter effect resulted in a "blaming the victim" dynamic. Woods workers perceived that they were being told (by outsiders, many politicians and political activists, and especially the media) that the crisis was of their own making. Further, that the only path to recovery was to abandon their occupation (often characterized as one which destroys nature) and its traditions. Barton's work indicates that blaming of victims in disaster situations is not uncommon:

> One factor that reduces sympathetic identification with the victims . . . is the development of explanations in which the victims themselves are held to blame for their own situation. Under what conditions is such an attitude to be found?
> Individually, we should expect to find such attitudes among those who accept highly moralistic and individualistic ideologies and values; among those with little contact with the victims; among those exposed to mass media content that explains that the victims are to blame; and among those whose social context is full of other people who blame the victims (Barton, 1970: 253-254).

The author also states that blaming of disaster victims is far less likely to be encountered in the case of sudden occurrences (i.e., fires, floods and wars) and more likely to be seen in instances where the onset of the disaster is less dramatic and the victims fall in a specific category:

> It is harder to stereotype sufferers if they come from all social categories. Large-scale suffering limited to one class or one ethnic group or one neighborhood is more easily related to prior stereotypes of moral or intellectual inferiority, which permit the victims to be held partly or entirely to blame (1970: 254).

Lifton and Olsen (1976) state that when disaster victims are ignored or blamed, they " . . . internalize . . . [a] . . . diminished sense of themselves." An example of this is found in the following quote taken from interview notes:

> _____ has no idea what he would do if he were not a logger. He said that he feels very attached to his occupation . . . [He] also says that he really doesn't know anything else, and that he's afraid that he's going to end up washing dishes or something because of his lack of educational background. He seemed very reluctant to talk about this, and . . . depressed about it. At one point he said that he couldn't help it that he was a dumb logger.
> [A logger's spouse] spoke [at length] about environmentalists and the media, and how they'[have] been putting forth stereotypes about loggers. She related a story about seeing a poster on the wall in the Sierra Club office when it was shown on television, [with] the poster [depicting] a picture of . . . "maniacal looking" loggers holding chain saws . . . [T]he caption at the bottom read: "The Washington Chain saw Massacre" . . . This made her really angry, and she [stated that] outsiders were really blaming loggers. She also mentioned that she felt that loggers were being portrayed as dim-witted, huge, bulky people that were pillaging the countryside.

The literature indicates further that the attributions that victims make concerning the cause of a disaster strongly reflect both their response and recovery. When a disaster is seen to have been caused by the conscious actions of other people, rather than impersonal forces such as nature, the reaction tends to be " . . . a sense of profound humiliation at the low value that seem[s] to [be] placed upon their lives "(Lifton and Olsen, 1976: 9). This reaction in the current case is exemplified in the following quote from an interviewee: ". . . especially the media has depicted us as if we were animals. Those of us living out here are human beings we have rights like other human beings."

The literature on human disasters and the interviews conducted for this study both indicate that the psychological impacts *vis a vis* culture and identity are likely to profoundly affect reactions to job impacts. To understand why this is different from reactions to economic downturns, it is important to recall that the loggers interviewed for both studies strongly embrace philosophical individualism such that they view market forces as more or less "natural," or at least beyond the control of any particular person or group. The owl issue on the other hand, was viewed by most loggers interviewed as a deliberate assault on their way of life. Lifton and Olsen (1976) note that damage to human personality is much more difficult to remedy when the causes are attributed to deliberate action on the part of others.

The long-term effects of the owl issue on loggers and their communities will not be known with any degree of certainty for a number of years. The extent to which the most potentially serious consequences of human disaster are eventually played out depends on a number of factors, including the actual timber allocations that eventually emerge, the specific timing of such allocations and their announcement, and the nature and extent of the help provided to various groups in the communities by federal programs and other sources. The long run prospects will be addressed in the final chapter. What can be said in summary, on the basis of this study, is that the "labor market adjustments" by loggers and their famalies in the affected communities studied are far more difficult and complicated than many have predicted.

8

The Future of Northwestern Loggers and Their Communities

One of the charges that can be leveled at case study research is that the results may be difficult to generalize directly to a larger population. The countervailing argument, of course, is that studies that are easily generalizable, particularly in the statistical sense, rarely go into the kind of depth necessary to uncover and understand underlying social processes (Gold, 1985; Blumer, 1969). The attempt here has been to achieve the latter objective.

No claims can, or will, be made that the specific results reported here fit every logging community or group of loggers in the region. Thus, any implications drawn for groups other than those specifically studied should be understood as bearing the the caveat "to the extent that the same social processes are operating". This is said, however, completely without apology, because, in keeping with the traditions of inductive sociological inquiry, other researchers are encouraged to conduct similar studies to build upon, modify, or take issue with the analysis presented here.

Secondly, the comparison of occupational community dynamics from the work of Hayner through the most recent impact studies appears to be building a strong case for the widespread existence and persistence of such patterns in western Washington, Oregon, and northern California. However, all of the studies reported on here were conducted in areas that were historically very timber-dependent. Thus it seems likely that the occupational community dynamics observed were at what might be described as their most highly developed. It would be very useful to interview loggers in locations closer to urban centers to observe differences. Finally, and most fundamentally, these studies are in no way intended to be the final word on loggers and logging communities. The studies discussed here have raised as many questions as they have answered, as is usual in such an understudied subject area. The latter portion of this chapter will be an attempt to raise or restate some of those questions to encourage others to join in the search for answers.

The primary research question asked in each of the two case studies has generated an amply definitive answer. The loggers interviewed and observed clearly fit the criteria to be characterized as members of an occupational community. Additionally, the dynamics of the occupational community, particularly with respect to identity and reputation, are important to understanding loggers' behavior in a rapidly changing world. The occupational identity, sense of independence, and job information networks characteristic of the loggers' occupational community have been sources of empowerment for its members and have historically allowed them to adapt to the seasonal and cyclic nature of the forest products economy. However, such features, have not prepared loggers particularly well for changes in the political economy that have, in combination, created significant short- and long-term uncertainty about their employability.

In the case of the question posed in the second study, the evidence clearly indicates that a simple labor market view of worker behavior in the face rapidly disappearing jobs does not begin to frame "the whole story". Rather, the timber issue (in conjunction, of course, with the historical, political, and economic changes that led up to it) was creating complex economic social and psychological effects on loggers and their families. The story of these effects can only be adequately told in light of the history and culture of the occupation, current occupational community dynamics, and the nature and sequence of events in the controversy itself. And, as we have noted, the story is far from over.

Some significant choices are faced concerning the future of loggers and their communities in the Northwest. It should also be noted that the circumstances and choices faced by these people appear to have many parallels to other rural groups in a rapidly changing national and global context. The main purposes of this chapter are to attempt to articulate some of these choices, revisit the subject of the broader social and economic context in which they are occurring, and to pose and/or restate some as yet unanswered questions about the dynamics that currently affect the lives, and will likely influence the destiny, of these workers and their families.

Before moving on to that discussion, however, a subject that deserves additional emphasis is the importance of looking beyond (and often within) the territorial community in the quest to understand the effects of resource policy decisions specifically on people with direct ties to lands and resources. The notion of occupational community may well be usefully applied to a variety of rural groups beyond loggers and commercial fishers perhaps including special forest product (i.e., mushroom, bear grass, and floral greens) harvesters, sheep herders, farm and ranch "hands", and perhaps even some specific groups of land owners. The "search for community", however, should go beyond territorial and occupational groupings to include a variety of ways people attach themselves to each other and to the land:

> Land managers must recognize more inclusive definitions of community and provide meaningful opportunities for the many public lands communities to share responsibility for the decisions that affect them. For their part, people who are part of the various communities are challenged to find a common language that expresses their shared concerns and to nurture a sense of ownership of a special place for which they care deeply (Bates, 1993: 111).

Perhaps the best analogy that can be applied to communities that have a stake in public lands is that of a varied mosaic not unlike the ecological mosaics described by forest ecologists: varied, changing, sometimes in competition, and nearly always colorful.

Implications and Choices

What implications can be drawn concerning the future prospects for Northwestern loggers as an occupational community? It is clear, as most commentators on the subject have stated, change is clearly inevitable. No group or community can ultimately be insulated from what the sociologist, Roland Warren (1987) terms the "vertical linkages" that extend from the larger society to local communities. It is suggested here, however, that the particular form such change takes is neither inevitable, nor is it driven exclusively by the "invisible hand" of predestined economic (or, for that matter, ecological) forces. The future of these workers and their communities hinges, in large part (as it always has) on political choices from a range of possibilities that are bounded by ecology, larger macroeconomic forces and policies and human culture. As we will suggest, that future will also be influenced by the way the circumstances faced by these people is symbolized in the larger society.

One such choice as we noted in Chapter 1, and which seems at this juncture to have been made, is a significant reduction in available public timber supply. While the specific magnitude of this reduction will likely be determined jointly (or at least approved) by the Executive Branch, the Courts, Congress, the various private and public interest groups, and the land management agencies, a return to the federal timber harvest levels planned in the pre-Spotted Owl era for the Douglas-fir region appears to be very unlikely. This precipitous reduction in availability of timber for harvest represents a dramatic shift in to federal land policy in at least two senses.

On the one hand, it represents the polar opposite of the recommendations frequently heard in the 1970s and early 1980s that, in the case of the national forests in the Northwest, managers should "depart" from non-declining even flow timber harvest regulation in order to *accelerate* the liquidation of "decadent" old-growth Douglas-fir to make way for second-growth stands. The other sense in which it represents a shift in policy is that its economic effect on at least some timber workers and communities is exactly what the advocates for sustained yield timber regulation argued throughout most of the century that federal timber policy should seek to *prevent* (Pinchot, 1972; Mason, 1927; Dana, 1917,1956; Drielsma, Miller, and Burch, 1990). The latter authors note sardonically:

> [T]he sustained yield idea of forestry is a valuable case. It is further confirmation that ideas directed to the benefit of lower social strata are most often controlled by upper social strata. Further, the rise and fall of such ideas are best predicted by understanding patterns in circulation of elites, rather than the increasing or decreasing misery of particular dependent populations or ecosystems (Drielsma, Miller, and Burch, 1990: 64).

The owl controversy itself emerged as a result of a complex interplay of the timing of public and private harvesting patterns, public agency behavior, the increased urbanization of U.S. society, interest group politics, the growth of ecological knowledge, and, most fundamentally of all, a shift in the dominance of particular culturally based ideas and images about the value of forests and their relationship to society (Buttel, 1992; Gregg, 1992; Wilkinson, 1992). As the ninth district federal judge who has presided over a number of judicial proceedings concerning this controversy, stated in a decision: "The fate of the Spotted Owl has become a battleground largely because the species is a symbol of the remaining old-growth forest" (Dwyer, 1991: 10).

Another significant aspect of the controversy that bears repeating is the fact that it was not the protection of ancient forests per se that triggered the difficulties looming in timber towns. Rather it was the timing and manner of decision-making that resulted in the most significant adverse impacts. If reductions in available stands for harvest had been decided even a decade or two in advance, incremental adjustments in public land harvests could have been made. Rapid *implementation* (as opposed to timely announcement) of harvest reductions, particularly as related to the effects of court injunctions, tends to exacerbate the negative impacts because those affected have little time to prepare.

Thus, the suddenness with which the issue finally came to a head (as opposed to the decades over which it had been building), the political brinkmanship and rancor with which it played out, and the perception on the part of workers that they were being blamed by the larger society for creating their own misery, all contributed the painful consequences experienced by loggers and others in the areas studied. It also bears repeating that the effects of this controversy should be understood in the context of broader political and economic changes that have been discussed in this volume.

Arguments suggesting that the difficulties faced in the communities are entirely the result of habitat protection, or are entirely due to other factors such as mechanization and "capital flight", are equally disingenuous. It is important to recall that forest product workers in the region were facing economic uncertainty and decline well before the owl. It is also significant to note that if the old-growth had continued to be harvested at the somewhat reduced rates called for in the forest plans, the harvest could have gone a long way to bridge the current "fiber gap" until forest industry lands come back on line in two to three decades. These statements should not be construed as an argument for or against habitat protection, but are made in an attempt to place the dispute in a reasonably balanced context.

It is also significant that, while the details of particular public land planning efforts have been subject to some local influence, the larger order decisions (such as how to structure public land planning processes, whether to "depart" from non-declining even flow in regulating national forest timber harvest, or whether or not to list the owl) have been far more directly influenced by formal, professionalized interest groups representing industry, environmentalists, and other national level political organizations. Loggers and others in the local communities have perceived that the political decisions that directly affect their lives are more or less out of their sphere of influence. (Only at the latter stages of the dispute did organized labor emerge as a highly visible player in the dispute. As we have seen, organized labor's relationship to some groups of woods workers is weaker than its ties to mill workers.)

Timber community activism related to the owl/old-growth issue and the emergence of the broader "wise use" movement in reaction to perceived excesses in federal environmental regulation throughout the West[1] altered this pattern to some extent, but the method of community influence on the larger land management issues remains largely outside "normal" channels, taking instead the form of media exposure, social protest, and direct appeals to Congress. While there are many reasons why locals perceive themselves to have had little influence, the net result for them is a sense of powerlessness and frustration. As we have seen, the study uncovered considerable evidence of political alienation on the part of loggers and some others in the affected local areas. Whether the torn political fabric can be mended in the post-owl crisis period is yet to be seen (Daniels,1992b).

Another set of political choices, and one which has implications far beyond the owl/forest issue, concerns the often discussed topic of economic diversification in forest-based local economies. While most commentators and analysts on all sides of the dispute agree that it is wise for rural economies to attempt to diversify, it is important to note that diversification could create as well as solve problems. In addition to the myriad of practical economic considerations (i.e., what kind of enterprises to attract or create? What kinds of resources and skills would be needed? Can this be done in time to help people who are already or soon to be out of work? Will the jobs pay enough to support a family?) looms the question of which local residents such efforts and enterprises would actually help. The evidence gathered in these studies suggests that diversification efforts, if carried out without the active participation of its intended beneficiaries, could increase the cultural conflicts already underway over the timber question.

One worker interviewed expressed concisely a sentiment held by many: "Personally, I'd rather starve to death here and live off elk meat rather than participate in any degrading plans to move me around and change my culture and life."

This reaction was found to be especially common among loggers, who felt particularly under attack as a result of the controversy anyway. From their perspective, it adds insult to injury to create economic opportunities that are more suited for others, while their livelihoods are disappearing as a result of decisions that they do not perceive as legitimate.

Questions of retraining face the same difficulties. In one of the study sites a sign was seen in a front yard with the inscription: "Retrain?? . . . If I'd wanted a CPA, I would have married one!!"

As a group, loggers appear to be among the least likely community residents to be readily amenable to participating in retraining efforts, particularly for occupations that, from their perspective, restrict personal freedom. Any efforts that smack of "social engineering" seem likely to be met with resentment by members of this group. This is not to suggest that some loggers will not opt for retraining, but serious questions remain about the long-term effects of retraining on this particular group, given its traditions and collective identity. This is a topic worthy of a time-series study.

External Influences

The changes in the lives of Northwestern loggers documented in the above chapters are clearly linked to the product of the larger economic, political, and social changes described in Chapter 1. The economic uncouplings and complexities described by Drucker (1986; 1994) and Carroll and Daniels (1992) noted in the first chapter have clearly resulted in economic decline and increased uncertainty in logging towns (Hibbard 1992). The owl controversy provides perhaps the clearest domestic example currently available of the patterns that Buttel (1992) describes. History may well show that the spotted owl dispute marked the clear emergence of the new political dynamics described by Buttel. The issue was a direct result of NSM activitism. The language in which the dispute has been argued is heavily scientized. Calls for the preservation of ancient forests represent a clear example of the transformation of scientific (in this case ecological) concepts into ethical claims that Buttel discusses.

In addition to the economic and political changes noted above, the evidence gathered and the events described in these studies lead us to suggest the existence of a third set of macro-level transformations that appear to be emerging in the current era. These changes may be described as "cultural uncoupling", as they create a growing rift between rural producers and (mostly) urban and ex-urban consumers of natural resource commodities. As we have seen, the spotted owl controversy was perceived by many in the study areas as fundamentally a cultural battle. The expressed sense of alienation from the "urban majority" and the accompanying perception that urbanites are both willfully ignorant and unconcerned about where their wood products originate and the consequences of the owl issue for rural workers are expressions of this uncoupling?

Battles, such as the one described here, seem destined to have long-term implications for the future of rural life. Although there is growing recognition of the uncoupling of rural and urban economies, as evidenced in the phrases "the two Oregons" or the "other Oregon" (Hibbard, 1989), less attention is paid to the growing cultural uncoupling. The implications of potentially long-term polarization or cultural segmentation of traditional rural groups on the future of rural governance, the provision and effectiveness of rural education and social services, the effectiveness of future rural economic development efforts, and the persistence of rural poverty are topics worthy of additional attention and analysis (Geisler, 1991; Carroll, 1991).

A related question pertaining to the long-term impacts of the owl issue (and more generally of recent trends in public land decision-making) on the political fabric in rural areas will have an impact as well. One author states:

> The owls/jobs dispute has become so rancorous that there is little or no prospect of a solution without legislative intervention at [the] national level. One of the unfortunate and overlooked aspects of this dispute is that there co-exists a large set of on-going management issues that must also be addressed [environmental disclosure documents pursuant to the National Environmental Policy Act . . . forest plans . . . etc.]. The polarization produced by the owl debate diverts attention from these issues, but it has also created a set of publics who view each other as little more than mortal enemies (Daniels, 1992b: 2).

The lines tend to be drawn, as we have seen, between those whose way of life is linked to make a living directly from the land versus those whose view of the forest is influenced by environmentalism. As Daniels (1992b) points out, what has not received as much attention is that the two groups tend to bring different culturally based definitions of standing to the decision processes. In describing a meeting of stakeholders concerning a national forest decision, he observed:

> All of the environmentalists described their interests in terms of either a desire to see various legal processes fulfilled or of the time they had spent studying the drainage. All but one [logging] representative expressed their standing as resulting from the number of generations they had lived in the area and/or the number of people depending on them for jobs. During the meeting both sides repeatedly implied or stated that the other side's position was not valid, particularly because that side had no standing (Daniels, 1992b: 12).

Related to this issue is the fact that traditional local rural people such as loggers tend to bring fewer political or organizational resources to the decision processes than do environmentalists or higher level lobbyists for industry (Daniels and Carroll, 1991). In the post-NEPA era of public land management planning, the art of influencing decision-making has become increasingly sophisticated. The ability to be eloquent before a microphone (or television camera), to write an appeal or a legal brief, and to understand and to stay current concerning complex planning procedures have become the currency needed to be fully effective in participating in (or in the latter case, even interpreting) land management decision processes. From a logger's perspective, for example, it seems that someone (probably from an urban area) can initiate an environmental action "over a lunch hour" and eliminate the logger's paycheck a few months hence.

While this example is clearly a stereotyped oversimplification of the way most group influence actually occurs, the point is that the decision-making processes as they have played out in recent years, have often tended to leave rural working class people feeling both disenfranchised and perceiving that they have been forced to absorb a disproportionate share of economic and political uncertainty. The following is taken from fieldnotes in the second study:

> _____ felt that the current restrictions were being put in place by "preservationists", whose motives and actions "go way beyond logic". He also stated that environmentalists never bring anything to the table, and that they don't make any compromises. He said that they'll propose a plan that benefits them completely, and then offer, as a compromise, that same plan, scaled back. He said that environmentalists never see a compromise as themselves sacrificing something in turn, as the timber communities will have to sacrifice something. He also expressed his concern that the media has been totally favoring and expressing the views of the "preservationists". He is also concerned that a lot of planning had been done that was reversed by the owl decision, and that caused a lot of cynicism among workers and owners in the timber industry. He felt that instead of being rewarded for having good planning and good management practices, they were punished by a politically-induced decision. He also felt that this affected private owners; that it was forcing all loggers and people who had bid for timber sales and small mills to cut early and cut quickly, because the future was so uncertain.

This situation is clearly not a recipe for productive citizenship or adaptive problem solving.

The patterns described here have striking parallels to conflicts involving environmentalists and animal rights activists versus trappers and seal hunters (both native and non-native) in Alaska and Canada (Wenzel, 1991), cattle ranchers versus advocates for removing cattle from public rangelands (Marston, 1992; Ferguson and Ferguson, 1983), and advocates for, versus local opponents to, federal river protection in inhabited rural areas (Carroll, 1988; Carroll and Hendrix, 1992).

The problems associated with these seemingly endless and often rancorous conflict over public land decision-making have generated increased attention in the literature. Julia Wondolleck (1988) suggests that national forest decisions be reconceptualized as disputes to be resolved, rather than decisions to be made solely by experts. She suggests further that procedures be designed to bring competing interests together with built-in mechanisms, such as joint fact finding to arrive at commonly acceptable decisions. Margaret Shannon has more recently (1991) suggested the need to build "Civic Friendship" and "Civic Conversation" in developing public land policy. Shannon goes on to point out that many rural cultures are oral and settle things "around the kitchen table". She calls for the development of institutions for public land decision-making that incorporate such traditions. Lee (1993) calls for the creation of a "Civic Science" to bring together scientific understanding and value based political decision-making to make decisions that are both technically sound and politically legitimate. The practical viability of a wholesale restructuring of land management decision-making to incorporate such ideas, and the potential of such innovations to heal the wounds of political and cultural divisions over public land questions, remain as open and very important questions.

An even larger related issue, concerns the dilemma of how to view the national interest *vis a vis* public lands in the current era. Gifford Pinchot's notion that in national forest decision-making "local questions should be solved on local grounds" has been called into question in the era of national and global interest groups competing over the disposition of these lands. One of the arguments frequently heard in federal land disputes is that local interests should receive no special consideration simply because of physical proximity to the lands. Yet there is the irony that the U.S. helps to support international forestry programs that are aimed, in large part, to make life better for local populations in other countries. Approaches such as transactive planning are used to help assure that local culture and knowledge are incorporated into such programs (Friedman, 1987).

The 1990 Farm bill included language that recognized the need for economic development assistance in U.S. rural communities, yet there seems currently to be no consensus about whether federal land decisions should consider in any specific way, the well being of adjacent rural populations (Society of American Foresters, 1989) or whether attempts should be made to more effectively involve rural people in decision processes that affect their lives (Carroll and Hendrix, 1992). The FEMAT report addressed these questions, but did so largely from the stand point of technocratic decision-making to be followed by social and economic mitigation for the affected communities more or less after-the-fact (Walker and Daniels, 1993).

Worker Adaptability: A Multi-Faceted Question

As we have noted, the Northwestern logger's world is clearly undergoing changes at least as dramatic as those described by Hayner in the transition from steam to gasoline technology. The current changes, as we have seen, are driven not only (or even primarily) by evolving technology, but by a variety of external political and economic changes that are probably not subject to complete understanding by means of any single analytic approach.

One issue that looms large is the meaning, or perhaps the dimensions, of the concept of adaptation as it is applied to the members of this particular occupation. The current studies, as well as others previously noted, lead to the conclusion that Northwestern loggers have historically been very adaptable, particularly with respect to solving technological problems. Under "normal" (or perhaps we should now say "historical") conditions, occupational networks in concert with personal reputations functioned in lieu of formal certification for matching employees with available jobs.

But what does adaptation mean in a time of great upheaval and uncertainty? One school of thought holds that retraining in dramatically different occupations, such as computer technology or a service field coupled with more or less simultaneous economic diversification in affected areas (or perhaps migration to urban areas), constitutes an adaptation strategy for displaced resource extraction workers. As we have suggested, this is unlikely to be a complete answer and could lead to an acceleration of social/cultural conflict, particularly if it were perceived by its intended recipients as social engineering from "without."

Thus, it becomes apparent that any conception of adaptation should be culturally located. What might appear to be rational or logical behavior from one perspective may not from another. The most striking example of this was the response of shake and shingle workers in one study area (briefly noted in the previous chapter) that moving away from home and family networks would be the "last thing" they would do in a time of economic stress. A further implication is that to remove the element of volunteerism from adaptation is to create a very different concept -- and one that has the potential to be used in a dehumanizing manner. Yaffee quotes from an interview with an Oregon environmental activist which provides a striking example of this:

> I personally look around at a lot of these loggers, and I feel sorry for
> them because of their lifestyle. They're uneducated, they're crude,
> they're not people I would choose to be around. I don't think there's a

> defensible reason to keep these people doing what they're doing and
> keep them in their state of ignorance. So I think that we need to find
> some forms of job retraining, and perhaps ways to educate them. Bring
> them up so they can spell, talk, and get along like the rest of us (Yaffee,
> 1994: 180).

In addition, it should be recalled that the literature on human disasters
suggests that people who perceive themselves to be suffering misfortune
as a result of actions by others more powerful than themselves tend not
to adapt (by any cultural definition) but to focus their energy on what
they view as the injustice committed and its perpetrators. The extent to
which this becomes a long-term pattern in logging communities remains
to be seen.[2]

Another dimension of this question concerns the strategies that will
lead to survival for those workers (and logging companies) who endure
into the "post-owl" era. How will the work be organized? Will a "new
breed" of loggers be needed to harvest trees in the era of changed
forestry practices? Research is currently being undertaken to begin to
anticipate the future demands for a forestry work force (Lee, 1992).
Anecdotal evidence suggests, for example, that attempts are being made
by logging contractors to develop more mechanized, high production
forest thinning operations to replace the (back breaking, typically low
paying) hand thinning operations of the past.

Finally, there is the question of whether (and how) the impetus for
environmental protection generally, and forest protection specifically,
can be extracted from the current cultural battle in which the interests of
loggers and other rural working people are pitted against protection in
rancorous contests of political brinkmanship. As Beverly Brown (1991)
points out, members of the rural working class have as big a stake as
anyone in the long-term sustainability of the forest ecosystems upon
which they have traditionally depended to make a living.

Finding approaches to decision-making and environmental
protection that emphasize both consensus building (over both
philosophical and practical matters) and cultural sensitivity would
appear to be in the interests of both environmental protection and the
well being of working people and others in rural areas. While this would
clearly be a very tall order, and would require significant political
rethinking, the alternative might be deeper and more enduring cultural
divisions, the potential for political backlash and, as Buttel (1992) notes,
the risk of the creation of a more or less permanent rural underclass.

If there is one dominant theme that runs through the data from the
two studies, it is the state of embattlement in which loggers find
themselves with respect to environmentalism and the barriers to

adaptability that their embattlement creates. This state appears to be to the benefit of neither the workers or the environmental movement. As Buttel (1992) states:

> Yet, I suspect that the path taken and consequences of greening will depend on how these concerns are articulated with social justice ones. [Environmentalism] will probably need to be tied to social justice in order to be enduring (Buttel, 1990: 16).

Conclusion

If one were asked to extract but two lessons from the studies and analysis presented in this volume, the first would be that the question of the adaptation of rural area workers and their families to changes resulting from the evolution of the world economy and the governmental institutions of western society, is not as simple as it might appear. The second lesson would be that the question of what constitutes a community in the context of a rural landscape is not straightforward either. The latter point is of more than just academic interest, because the entities to which individuals look for their identity sense of belonging and security are very important in shaping adaptive behavior. Our society faces a number of trends that we cannot readily alter, yet there are a variety of choices to be made about the future of the management and allocation of natural resources. The choices made will have a direct impact on the direction of those trends, as well as upon the various kinds of human communities that depend directly and indirectly on the resource base. As Lee, Burch, and Field note, "These trends suggest that human community, organization and participation and values will become an even more essential component of future forest and natural resource planning and management" (1990: 288). It is hoped that this volume will contribute to a richer understanding of the consequences of such planning and management for rural residents, workers, and their families, all of whom feel the effects of such trends very directly.

Notes

1. The emergence of the wise use movement is a subject beyond the scope of this volume, but one worthy of scholarly attention.

2. It should be noted, however, that there appeared to be a noticeable difference in loggers' attitudes toward education for their children between the two studies. Almost without exception, loggers and their spouses in the later study said that they were encouraging their children to become well educated in

order to have more options in life than they have had. The extent to which this encouragement leads to concrete action and a truly different way of life for the children of logging families and what consequences might flow from such an occurrence, is an intriguing issue that also deserves further attention.

Epilogue

The research that has been described in this book can be argued to have implications for (or at least linkages to) a number of policy questions and dilemmas that remain unresolved as of this writing. The purpose of this epilogue is to present a very brief series of vignettes in which a portion of those implications and unanswered questions are noted.

Retraining

One of the issues that has been raised time and again in the debates over the social impacts of timber harvest reduction concerns the extent to which such impacts can be mitigated by retraining displaced workers. The literature on job retraining suggests a mixed track record, at best, for large scale retraining efforts (Leigh, 1990). A central issue for loggers revolves around identity transformation and attachment to the land and a rural way of life. Compounding this, of course, is the anger and sense of alienation resulting from the forest controversy.

Careful thought and planning about realistic employment opportunities, planning which takes account of their existing skills, knowledge, and "hands on" orientation appears to be called for. Nothing would be more alienating to such workers than being offered training for which there are no jobs, or being asked to develop skills that are completely alien to their culture and way of life. Any retraining programs should be carefully monitored, and adjustments made, if the retraining falls short in its attempt to increase the life chances of enrollees.

Ecological Restoration Employment

Much was said at the President's Forest Conference about the need for ecological restoration and the potential for government ecological restoration projects to employ displaced forest workers. The topic not broached was how such work would be organized and carried out. Some experimentation is probably in order to attempt to find effective ways to conduct restoration activities.

Given the importance of independence in the culture of logging and the widespread cynicism among loggers about bureaucratic organization of work, it would probably make sense to organize at least a portion of such activities on a product rather than an hourly wage basis. One difficulty, of course, would be to establish quality standards and agreed-upon units of production. Another issue will be the selection of workers. If preference is given to displaced timber workers, will the current definitions used by state employment agencies be used? Within those definitions, should prior experience in particular jobs such as falling and equipment operation be counted? Who will supervise such work? Will it be contracted or will workers be federal employees? Such questions are important, not only from the standpoint of efficiency, but also from the standpoint of whether many loggers can "live" within such a system. Given the difficulties and the inherently temporary nature of restoration work, it appears that such activities, at best, will only solve a small part of the forest worker displacement problem.

Community Assistance Programs

The social analysis carried out as a part of FEMAT pointed out that three aspects of community life are linked to the impacts of timber harvest reduction. These are physical infrastructure, human capital, and a concept labeled "civic responsiveness." As Daniels (1994) notes, the early programs developed by the Clinton administration emphasized the first category (i.e., "bricks and mortar" projects). He challanges policy makers to think about how to develop projects that both provide assistance to displaced individuals and foster involvement of a variety of groups within geographic communities. He goes on to suggest that such projects be funded not with annual appropriations, but by means of a trust fund to be created and then drawn down over a period roughly coinciding with the coming "on line" of the industrial timber base in the region.

Whether such an approach proves politically possible, the larger point is that assistance should not simply be thought of simply in terms of the physical attributes of towns, but should take into account the social dynamics and the particular groups (notably displaced workers and their families) within affected areas most in need of assistance. To fail to do so would be to add to the sense of disenfranchisement already felt by many in such places.

National "Versus" Local Interests:
The Need to Move Beyond the Divisive Dichotomy

On a broader level, one important lesson from the owl controversy is the high cost in terms of political polarization (and its many negative effects) stemming from framing debates about public lands in terms of local versus national interests. This kind of thinking creates what sociologist/policy analyst David Freeman (1992) terms "polarized cleavages" that do not encourage proponents on either side of public land issues to grant standing to those who hold other points of view as a first step in attempting to resolve such disputes. Speaking of similar issues in another region in the West, Kemmis writes:

> The Northern Rockies states all have vast stretches of federally owned land, and for over a decade now they and the nation itself, have been embroiled in a seemingly endless process of deciding how much of that land to designate as protected wilderness. That debate pits various interests . . . against each other in a standoff struggle which has sapped the energy and resources of all concerned. At the same time, this struggle has gradually undermined nearly all parties' faith that the process of public decision-making is in fact capable of identifying or producing the public interest (Kemmis, 1990: 39 emphasis added).

In the case of the owl controversy (as in wilderness questions and many other public land issues) the political equation that has often emerged holds environmental protection as being primarily a matter of national interest and the viability of local economies, cultures, and social systems as reflecting only the local interest. What this equation fails to account for is the interest of local rural populations in the sustainability of forests around them and the national interest in the existence of healthy local communities and economies. This also ignores linkages between cultural diversity and bio-diversity (Snyder, 1993). While none of this is meant to minimize the very real value conflicts described in this volume, it does suggest that there are more productive ways to frame public land issues.

One set of ideas which holds promise in helping to re-frame such issues goes by a number of labels in the literature including "the new localism," "the new regionalism," and "the politics of place." The central ideas common to this literature (which are perhaps most completely and clearly articulated in Kemmis (1990) are the need to both broaden *and* localize decision-making. On the need to broaden decision-making, Brandenburg (1994) states:

. . . when seeking to understand attitudes, values, emotions and preferences regarding resource use . . . research indicates that traditional planning processes and tools are often less than adequate in capturing the variety of stakeholder's opinions. . . . Therefore, the complexities of human communities that are linked to forests in a variety of ways are not captured and many of the "voices" that speak for the forest are lost (Brandenburg, 1994: 42).

On the need to localize decisions Kemmis writes:

It is not simply that they [stakeholders concerning a national forest management plan] are expected to to present adversarial cases to a neutral third party, but to a "fed"-- to a representative of a remote, powerful government which owns most of the land and resources upon which their livelihood and well-being depend.

It would be an insult to these people to to assume that they are incapable of reaching some accomodation among themselves about how to inhabit their own place. Such accommodation would never be easy, and it would probably always be open to some redefinition. But if they were allowed to solve their own problems (and manage their resources) themselves, they would soon discover that no one wants local sawmills closed, and no one wants wildlife habitat annihilated. If encouraged to collaborate, they would learn to inhabitat the place on the place's own terms better than any regulatory bureaucracy will ever accomplish (Kemmis, 1990: 126-127).

Kemmis might be accused of being a bit utopian about local peoples' ability to easily organize decision processes when valuable resources are being contested. He is also perhaps excessively hard on bureaucracies (in fairness, he is equally hard on absentee business interests); however, his ideas about locating land management decision-making at levels at which its consequences will be felt and lived with are worth taking seriously. Such is not necessarily an argument for removing the federal government from the land management picture and would certainly not entail ignoring large scale ecological processes (or for that matter world markets). Rather, it can be taken as a perspective for reconsidering the appropriate scale at which particular decisions are made and for rethinking how to involve affected stakeholders. Such a perspective *would* probably lead one to search for alternatives to negotiating Allowable Sale Quantities for national forest timber sales in Senators' offices in Washington, D.C., and for determining the boundaries of special management areas from the map tables in regional offices of federal agencies.

The Need for Collaboration

If the reader is left with no other impression about the social impacts of the owl/forest issue, it should be clear that the controversy has torn the fabric of trust between many groups in the region. What began as a dispute ostensibly over an obscure species of bird escalated into a national battle, seen by some groups as a cultural battle with a multi-generational way of life at stake and by others as the last chance to save an ecosystem on the verge of final destruction. If a long-term balkanization of many groups in the region is to be avoided, positive steps should be taken to repair damaged relationships and decision processes. Much has been written in the natural resource and the social science literatures about building and maintaining collaborative relationships and it is not the intention to review that literature here. However, a strong case can be made for bottom up rather than top down approaches to both community mitigation and the myriad of specific resource allocation decisions that will be made within the general forest management framework that eventually emerges.

As Charles Wilkinson (1992) suggests, to be successful and humane, future resource decision-making should respect cultural and value differences and promote tolerance rather than attempting to "homogenize" groups with attachments to the land. As ecologists have described the mosaic of ecological relationships across the landscape, so it is social groups as well. As Daniels (1994) suggests, one place to begin in the present context is to find ways to "re-value" labor in both an economic and political sense to counteract the vilification of loggers and other forest workers that occurred in the heat of the forest controversy. As part of such an effort, it would be important to re-examine widely held assumptions about the "inevitability" of "transformations" in forest communities and separate the very real need for adaptation to systemic changes which are beyond the control of any group or institution from deliberately induced cultural "transformation" imposed by one group upon another. It is the perception of cultural elitism that has been partially responsible for the often nasty political conflicts that have developed between rural "wise use" groups and environmentalists and government regulators over the owl and other public land issues. It appears that this dynamic must be addressed before collaborative decision-making can take place in many settings.

REFERENCES

Adams, Darius M., and Richard W. Haines. 1990. Public Policies, Private Resources, and the Future of the Douglas-Fir Region Forest Economy. *Western Journal of Applied Forestry*. 5, 3: 64-69.

Banton, M. 1964. *The Policeman in the Community*. London: Tavistock.

Barton, Allen H. 1970. *Communities in Disaster. A Sociological Analysis of Collective Stress Situations*. Garden City, New Jersey: Doubleday.

Bates, Sarah. 1993. Public Lands: Communities in Search of a Community of Values. *Public Land Law Review*. 14: 81-112.

Becker, Howard S and Anselm Strauss. 1967. Careers, Personality and Adult Socialization. *American J. Sociology*. 62: 253-263.

Becker, Howard S. 1951. The Professional Dance Musician and His Audience. *American J. of Sociology*. LVII: 137.

_____. 1963. Outsiders. New York: The Free Press.

Becker, Howard S. and James Carper. 1956. The Elements of Identification with an Occupation. *American Sociological Review*. 21: 341-348.

Behan, R.W. 1966. The Myth of the Omnipotent Forester. *Journal of Forestry*. 64,6: 398-400,407.

_____. 1978. Political Popularity and Conceptual Nonsense: The Strange Case of Sustained Yield Forestry. *Environmental Law*. 8: 309-342.

_____. 1991. Forests and Plantations and Potomo-Centric Statutory Fixes. *Forest Perspectives*. 1(1): 5-8.

Bender, Thomas. 1978. *Community and Social Change in America*. Baltimore: The Johns Hopkins University Press.

Berger, Peter L. and Thomas Luckmann. 1967. *The Social Construction of Reality: A Treatise in the Sociology of Knowledge*. Garden City, New York: Anchor Books.

Beuter, John H. 1990. *Social and Economic Impacts in Washington, Oregon and California Associated with Implementing the Conservation Strategy for the Northern Spotted Owl: An Overview*. Washington, D.C.: American Forest Resource Alliance. (Cited in USDA Forest Service, 1992a).

Blahna, Dale J. 1990. Social Bases for Resource Conflicts in Areas of Reverse Migration. *In* Lee Field and Burch. *Community and Forestry*, pp.159-178.

Blauner, R. 1960. Work Satisfaction and Industrial Trends in Modern Society *In* W. Galenson and S.M. Lipset (eds.) *Labor and Trade Unionism*. New York: Wiley, pp. 339-360.

Bledsoe,Stewart. 1989. We Are Working Differently and Better. *In* LeMaster, Dennis C. and John H. Beuter (eds). *Community Stability in Forest Based Economies*. Portland, Oregon: Timber Press.

Blumer, Herbert. 1969. *Symbolic Interactionism*. Englewood Cliffs, New Jersey: Prentice Hall.

Borman, Katherine, Margaret Lee Compte, and Judith Gotez. 1986. Ethnographic And Qualitative Research Design And Why It Doesn't Work. *American Behavioral Scientist*, 30,1: 42-57.

Bott, Elizabeth. 1957. *Family and Social Network: Roles, Norms and External Relationships in Ordinary Urban Families*. London: Travistock.

Brandenburg, Andrea M. 1994. *The Voices of Forest Places*. Master of Science Thesis. Department of Natural Resource Sciences. Washington State University, Pullman Washington.

Brennan, T., E.W. Cooney and H. Pollins. 1954. *Social Change in South West Wales.* London: Watts.

Brown, Beverly A. (In Press) *In Timber Country: Working People's Stories of Environmental Conflict and Urban Flight.* Boston: Temple University Press.

Brown, Beverly A 1991. Notes on Social and Economic Transformations in Southwest Oregon Paper presented at Poor Women in Timber Country, A Workshop in the Northwest Women's Studies Association Meeting, Washington State University, Pullman, Washington, 28pp.

Brown, Richard and Peter Brannen. 1970a. Social Relations and Social Perspectives Amongst Shipbuilding Workers -- A Preliminary Statement. Part one. *Sociology*. 4: 71-84.

_____. 1970b. Social Relations and Social Perspectives Amongst Shipbuilding Workers -- A Preliminary Statement. Part two. *Sociology*,. 4: 197-211.

Bulmer, Martin. 1975. Sociological Models of the Mining Community. *The Sociological Review.* 23, 1: 61-92.

Burrell, Gibson, and Gareth Morgan. 1985. *Sociological Paradigms And Organizational Analysis.* Pourtsmouth, New Hampshire: Heinemann Educational Books.

Burt, R. 1980. Models of Network Structure. *Ann. Rev. Sociol.* 6: 79-141.

Buttel, Frederick H. 1992. Environmentalization: Origins, Processes and Implications for Rural Social Change. *Rural Sciology*. 57,1: 1-27.

Byron, R.N. 1977. Community Stability and Forest Policy in British Columbia. *Canadian J. Forestry Research.* 8: 61-66.

Cannon, I.C. 1967. Ideology and Occupational Community: A Study of Compositors. *Sociology.* 1: 165-185.

Carroll, M. S. and W. G. Hendrix. 1992. Planning for Federally Protected Rivers: The Critical Need for Effective Local Involvement. *The Journal of the American Planning Association.* 58 (3): 346-352

Carroll, M.S. and S.E. Daniels. 1992. Public Land Management and Three Decades of Social Change: Thoughts on the Future of Public Lands and Public Demands. *In* Congressional Research Service, Library of Congress. *Multiple Use and Sustained Yield: Changing Philosophies For Federal Land Management.* Committee on Interior and Insular Affairs, U.S. House of Representatives, Committee Print No. 11. pp.45-86.

Carroll, Matthew S. 1988. A Tale of Two Rivers: Comparing NPS-Local Interaction in Two Areas. *Society and Natural Resources.* 1;4: 9-25.

_____. 1991. Northwestern Loggers: An Occupational Community at Risk in the Forest Management Wars. Paper Presented at the Annual Meeting of the Rural Sociological Society. Columbus, Ohio. August 19.

Clary, David M. 1986. *Timber and the Forest Service.* Lawrence, Kansas: University Press of Nebraska.

Clawson, Marion. 1979. Forests in the Long Sweep of American History. *Science.* 204: 1168-1174.

Cleaves,David. 1991. *Log Exports From Oregon: Domestic Conflict In An International Context.* Oregon State University Extension Service. EM 8461.

Colfer, J. Pierce and A. Michael Colfer. 1978. Inside Bushler Bay: Lifeways in Counterpoint. *Rural Sociology*. 43,2: 204-220.

Conway, Flaxen D. L. and Gail Wells. 1994. Timber in Oregon: History & Projected Trends. Extension Miscellaneous Bulletin 8544. Oregon State University, Corvallis Oregon. 16pp.

164

Cox, Thomas. 1974. *Mills And Markets: A History of the Pacific Coast Lumber Industry to 1900.* Seattle: University of Washington Press.
Cronon, William. 1991. *Nature's Metropolis: Chicago and the Great West.* New York: W.W. Norton and Company.
Dana, Samuel T. and Sally K. Fairfax. 1981. *Forest and Range Policy; Its Development in the United States.* Second Edition. New York: McGraw Hill.
Dana, Samuel T. 1917. A Forest Tragedy: The Rise and Fall of a Lumber Town. *Munsey's Magazine.* 60: 353-363 (Cited in Drielsma et al., 1990).
_____. 1956. *Forest And Range Policy: Its Development in the United States.* New York. McGraw-Hill.
Daniels, Steven E 1992a. Personal Correspondence. Department of Forest Resources, Oregon State University, Corvallis, Oregon.
_____. 1992b. Local Dispute Resolution Efforts and National Controversy: An Exploratory Analysis. Unpublished Manuscript. Department of Forest Resources, Corvallis: Oregon State University.
_____. 1994. A Framework for Discussion: Re-thinking Community Assistance. Unpublished Manuscript, Department of Forest Resources, Corvallis: Oregon State University.
Daniels, Steven E. and Matthew S. Carroll. 1991. Status Group Differences and Formalized Public Involvement as Barriers to Dispute Resolution. Paper presented at the Fourth North American Symposium on Society and Resource Management. Madison, Wisconsin. May 17-20.
Davis, Dona Lee. 1986. Occupational Community And Fishermen's Wives In A Newfoundland Fishing Village. *Anthropological Quarterly.* 59,3: 129-142.
Davis, Kenneth P. 1963. Conflict and Cooperation Among Trawler-men. *British Journal of Industrial Relations.* 1: 331-347.
Denzin, Norman K. 1992. Symbolic Interactionism and Cultural Studies. The Politics of Interpretation. Cambridge, MA: Blackwell Publishers.
Drielsma, Johannes H. Joseph A. Miller and William R. Burch Jr. 1990. Sustained Yield And Community Stability In American Forestry. *In* Lee, Field and Burch. *Community and Forestry*, pp.55-68.
Drucker, Peter F. 1986. The Changed World Economy. *Foreign Affairs.* 64,4: 768-791.
_____. 1994. Trade Lessons from the World Economy. *Foreign Affairs.* 73, 1: 99-108.
Drushka, Ken. 1990. The New Forestry: A Middle Ground in the Debate Over How to Manage the Regions Forests? *The New Pacific.* (Fall): 7-23.
Dwyer, W.L. 1991. Seattle Audubon Society, et.al. v. John L. Evans, et al. and Washington Contract Loggers Association et al., United States District Court, Western District of Washington. No. C89-160WD.
Ellis, Carolyn. 1986. *Fisher Folk: Two Communities on Chesapeake Bay.* Lexington KY. The University Press of Kentucky.
Easterbrook, Greg. 1994. The Birds. *New Republic.* 4132 (March 28): 22-29.
Ferguson, Denzel and Nancy Ferguson. 1983. *Scared Cows At The Public Trough.* Bend Oregon. Maverick Publications.
Ficken, Robert E. 1987. *The Forested Land: A History of Lumbering in Western Washington.* Seattle: University of Washington Press.
Fielding, Nigel G. 1986. Evaluating The Role Of Training In Police Socialization: A British Example. *Journal of Community Psychology.* 14,3: 319-330.

Fine, Gary A. 1990. Symbolic Interactionin a Post-Blumerian Age. *In* Ritzer, George (ed). *Frontiers of Social Theory: The New Synthesis.* New York. Columbia University Press. pp. 117-157.

_____. 1993. The Sad Demise, Mysterious Disappearance, and Glorious Triumph of Symbolic Interactionism. Annual Review of Sociology,. 19: 61-87.

Fitchen, Janet. 1991. Endangered Spaces, Enduring Places. Boulder, CO: Westview Press.

Force, Jo Ellen, Gary E. Machlis, Lianjun Zhang and Ann Kearney. 1993. The Relationship Between Timber Production, Local Historical Events, and Community Social Change: A Quantitative Case Study. *Forest Science,.* 39(4): 722-742.

Forest Ecosystem Management Assessment Team. 1993. *Forest Ecosystem Management: An Ecological, Economic, and Social Assessment.* U. S. Government Printing Office. (1993-793-071)

Fortmann, L. and J. Kusel. 1990. New Voices, Old Beliefs: Forest Environmentalism Among New and Longstanding Residents. *Rural Sociology.* 55(2): 214-232.

Freeman, David M. 1992. *Choice Against Choice: Constructing a Policy Assessment Sociology for Social Development.* Niwot, Colorado: The University Press of Colorado.

Friedman, E.A. and W. Havinghurst. 1954. The Meaning of Work and Retirement. Chicago: University of Chicago Press.

Friedmann, John. 1973. *Retracking America: A Theory of Transactive Planning.* Garden City, New Jersey: Anchor Books.

Gaventa, John. 1980. *Power and Powerlessness: Quiesence And Rebellion in an Applachian Valley.* Urbana Illinois. University of Illinois Press.

Geisler, Charles C. 1991. Insights and Oversights: Land Alienation and Poverty in the United States. Paper Presented at the Annual Meeting of the Rural Sociological Society. Columbus, Ohio. August 19.

Gerstl, J.E. 1961. Determinants of Occupational Community in High Status Occupations. *Sociological Quarterly.* 2: 37-48.

Glaser, Barney G. and Anselm L. Strauss. 1980. *The Discovery of Grounded Theory: Strategies for Qualitative Research.* New York: Aldine Publishing Company.

Gold, R.L. 1985. *Ranching, Mining and the Human Impact of Natural Resource Development.* New Brunswick, New Jersey: Transaction.

Gorte, Ross W. 1992. Economic Impacts of Protecting Spotted Owls: A Comparison and Analysis of Existing Studies. Washington, D.C.: The Library of Congress, Congressional Research Service.

Gould, Earnest. 1960. Fifty Years of Management at the Harvard Forest. *Harvard Forest Bulletin,* p. 29.

_____. 1964. The Future of Forests in Society. *Forestry Chronicle.* 40: 431-44.

Granovetter, Mark S. 1974. *Getting a Job: A Study of Contacts and Careers.* Cambridge: Harvard University Press.

Greber, Brian J. 1993. Impacts of Technological Change on Employment in the Timber Industries of the Pacific Northwest. *Western Journal of Applied Forestry.* 8, 1: 34-37.

Greber, B.J., and K.N. Johnson. 1991. What's all the debate about overcutting? *Journal of Forestry.* 89(11): 25-30.

Gregg, N. Taylor. 1992. Sustainability and Politics: The Cultural Connection. *Journal of Forestry..* 90,7: 17-21.

Gutierrez, R.J. 1985. Information and Research Needs for Spotted Owl Management. *In* R.J. Gutierrez and A.B. Cary (eds). *Ecology and Management of the Spotted Owl in the Northwest*. USDA Forest Service General Technical Report. PNW-185: 115-119.

Harbison, John S. 1991. Hard Times in the Softwoods: Contract Terms, Performance, and Relational Interests in National Forest Timber Sales. *Environmental Law*. 21,3: 863-909.

Harry, Joseph. 1969. Causes Of Contemporary Environmentalism. *Humboldt Journal of Social Relations*. 2,1: 1-7.

Hayner, Norman. 1945. Taming the Lumberjack. *American Sociological Review*. X(2): 217-225.

Hays, Samuel P. 1959. Conservation and the Gospel of Efficiency. New York: Antheneum.

_____. 1987. Beauty, Health and Permanence. Environmental Politics in the United States, 1955-1985. Cambridge: Cambridge University Press.

Healy, Robert G. 1984. Forest in Urban Civilization. Land Use, Land Markets, Ownership and Recent Trends. *In Changing Environment: The Urban Forest Interface*. Seattle: University of Washington Press. p. 17-35.

Hibbard, Michael. 1989. Issues And Options for the Other Oregon. *Community Development Journal*. 24,2: 145-153.

_____. 1992. Economic Culture and Responses to Economic Transformation in a Timber Dependent Community. *In Small Towns: Culture Change and Cooperation*. Denver, CO: The Western Governors' Association.

Hibbard, Michael and James Elias. 1993. The Failure of Sustained Yield Forestry and the Decline of the Flannel Shirt Frontier. *In* Thomas A. Lyson and William Falk (eds) *Forgotton Places: Uneven Development in Rural America*. Lawrence, Kansas. University Press of Kansas. pp. 195-217.

Hillery, George A. 1982. *A Research Odyssey. Developing And Testing A Community Theory*. New Brunswick, New Jersey: Transaction Books.

Hirt, Paul W. 1994. *A Conspiracy of Optimism: Management of the National Forests Since World War Two*. Lincoln, Nebraska. University of Nebraska Press.

Holbrook, Stewart H. 1926. The Logging Camp Loses its Soul. *Sunset*. (June): 19-21, 62-65.

_____. 1938. *Holy Old Mackinaw: A Natural History of the American Lumberjack*. New York: The Macmillan Company.

Hollowell, P.G. 1968. *The Lorry Driver*. London: Routledge and Kegan Paul.

Horobin, G.W. 1957. Community and Occupation in the Hull Fishing Industry. *British J. of Sociology*. 8: 343-356.

Hughs, Everett C. 1971. *The Sociological Eye.*. Selected Papers. New York: Aldine-Atherton.

Humphrey, C. R., G. Berardi, M. S. Carroll, S. K. Fairfax, L. Fortmann, C. Geisler, T. G. Johnson, J. Kusel, R. G. Lee, S. Macinko, M. D. Schulman, and P. C. West. 1993. Theories in the Study of Natural Resource-Dependent Communities and Persistant Rural Poverty in the United States. *In* Rural Sociological Society Task Force on Persistent Rural Poverty. *Persistent Poverty in Rural America*.. Boulder: Westview Press. pp.136-172.

Hyde, William F. 1980. *Timber Supply, Land Allocation, and Efficiency*. Baltimore: Resources for the Future, The Johns Hopkins Press.

Jackson, David H. and Patrick J. Flowers. 1983. The National Forests and Stabilization. *Western Wildlands* 8;4: 20-27.

Janowitz, M. 1960. The Professional Soldier. Glenroe, Illinios: The Free Press.

Johnston, Bryan M. and Paul J. Krupin. 1991. The 1989 Pacific Northwest Timber Compromise: An Environmental Dispute Resolution Case Study of a Successful Battle That May Have Lost the War. *Willamette Law Review*. 27,3: 613-643.

Kaufman, Herbert. 1953. Forest Use and Community Stability. *In* William.A. Duerr and H.enry J. Vaux (eds) *Research in the Economics of Forestry*. Washington, D.C.: Charles Lithrop Pack Foundation. pp. 113-119.

_____. 1960. *The Forest Ranger*. Baltimore. Johns Hopkins University Press.

Kemmis, Daniel. 1990. *Community and the Politics of Place*. Norman, Oklahoma: University of Oklahoma Press.

Koberstein, Paul. 1994. Spotted Owl May Be Loosing Its Long Fight For Survival. *High Country News*. 26(11): 1, 10-12.

Krannich and Luloff. 1991. Problems of Resource Dependency in U. S. Rural Communities. *In*: A.W. Gilg, D. Briggs, R. Dilley, O. Furuseth, and G. McDonald (eds). *Progress in Rural Policy and Planning*. Vol 1. New York. Belhaven Press. pp. 5-18.

Lacey, Michael J. 1979. *The Mysteries of Earthmaking Dissolve: A Study of Washington's Intellectual Community and the Origins of Environmentalism in the Late Nineteenth Century*. Ph.D Dissertation. Washington, D.C.: George Washington University.

Lee, Kia N. 1993. *Compass and Gyroscope: Integrating Science and Politics for the Environment*. Washington, D.C.: Island Press.

Lee, Robert G. 1977. Review Of Glenn Robinson's The Forest Service: A Study in Public Land Management. *In Harvard Journal On Legislation* 10 (Winter): 172-187.

_____. 1982. The classical sustained yield concept: content and philosophical origins. *In* LeMaster, Dennis, David Baumgartner and David Adams (eds.) *Sustained Yield*. (Proceedings). Washington State University, Pullman, WA.

Lee, Robert G. 1984. Sustained yield and social order. *In* H. K. Steen (ed). History of sustained yield forestry: A Symposium. Santa Cruz, Calif: Forest History Society.

_____. 1990. Sustained Yield and Social Order. *In* Lee Field and Burch. *Community and Forestry*.

_____. 1991a. Four Myths of Interface Communities. *Journal of Forestry*. 89 (6): 35-38.

_____. 1991b. Moral Exclusion and Rural Poverty: Myth Management and Wood Production Workers. Paper Presented at the Annual Meeting of the Rural Sociological Society. Columbus, Ohio. August 19.

_____. 1992. Personal correspondence. College of Forest Resources., University of Washington, Seattle.

Lee, Robert G., Matthew S. Carroll, and Kristin. K. Warren. 1991. The Social Impact of Timber Harvest Reductions in Washington State. *In* P Sommers and H. Birss. *Revitalizing the Timber Dependent Regions of Washington*. Northwest Policy Center, Seattle: University of Washington.

Lee, Robert G., P. Sommers, H. Birss, C. Nasser and J. Zientek. 1991. *Social Impacts of Alternative Timber Harvest Reductions on Federal Lands in O and C Counties*. College of Forest Resources and The North West Policy Center, Seattle: University of Washington.

Lee. Robert G., Donald R. Field and William R Burch, Jr. 1990. *Community and Forestry: Continuities in the Sociology of Natural Resources*. Boulder, Colorado: Westview Press.

168

Leigh, Duane E. 1990. *Does Retraining Work for Displaced Workers? A Survey of Existing Evidence*. Kalamazoo, Michigan: W.E. Upjohn Institute for Employment Research.

LeMaster, Dennis E. 1984. *Decade of Change: The Remaking of Forest Service Authority During the 1970s*. Westport Connecticut: Greenwood Press.

Lifton, Robert Jay and Eric Olsen. 1976. The Human Meaning Of Total Disaster: The Buffalo Creek Experience. *Psychiatry*. 39: 1-18.

Limerick, Patricia. 1987. *The Legacy of Conquest: The Unbroken Past of the American West*. New York: W.W. Norton.

Lipset, Seymour M., Martin A. Trow and James S. Coleman. 1956. *Union Democracy:: The Internal Politics of the International Typographical Union*.. Glencoe, Illinios. The Free Press.

Lucia, Ellis. 1975. *The Big Woods: Lumbering and Logging from Bull Teams to Helicopters in the Pacific Northwest*. New York: Doubleday.

Lummis, Trevor. 1977. The Occupational Community of East Anglican Fishermen: An Historical Dimension Through Oral Evidence. *British J. of Sociology*. 28,1: 51-74.

Machlis, Gary. E. and Jo Ellen Force. 1988. Community stability and timber-dependent communities. *Rural Sociology*. 53(2): 220-234.

Machlis, Gary E., Jo Ellen Force and Randy Guy Balice. 1990. Timber, Minerals and Social Change: An Exploratory Test of Two Resource Dependent Communities. *Rural Sociology*. 55(3): 411-424.

Marston, Ed. 1992. A Neighborly Approach to Sustainable Public-Land Grazing. *High Country News*. 24,5: 6-27.

Mason, D. T. 1927. Sustained Yield and American Forest Problems. *Journal of Forestry*. 16: 210-224.

McCall, George J. and J. L. Simmons. 1978. *Identities and Interactions: An Examination of Human Associations in Everyday Life*. New York: The Free Press.

Mead, George Herbert. 1934. *Mind, Self, and Society*. Chicago: University of Chicago Press.

Merton, Robert K. 1957. *Social Theory and Social Structure*. New York: The Free Press.

Meyer, H. Arthur, Arthur B. Recknagel, Donald Stevenson, and Ronald Bartoo. 1961. *Forest Management*. New York: The Ronald Press.

Milbrath, Lester W. 1985. Culture and the Environment in the United States. *Environmental Management*. 9(2): 161-172.

Miller, Mark L. and Jeffery C. Johnson. 1981. Hard Work and Cometition in the Bristol Bay Salmon Fishery. *Human Organization*. 40,2: 131-139.

Moore, Roberts. 1975. Religion as a Source of Variation in Working-Class Images of Society. *In* Martin Bulmer (ed) *Working Class Images of Society*. London and Boston: Routledge and Kegan Paul. p. 35-54.

Morrison, Peter H. 1988. *Old Growth in the Pacific Northwest: A Status Report*. Washington D.C.: The Wilderness Society.

Muth, Robert C. 1990. Community Stability as Social Structure: The Role of Subsistence Uses of Natural Resources in Southeast Alaska. *In* Lee Field and Burch. *Community and Forestry*.

Nash. Roderick. 1973. *Wilderness and the American Mind*. New Haven: Yale University Press.

Nelson, Joel I. and Robert Grams. 1978a. Worker Interaction in Occupational Communities. *Rural Sociology*. 43,2: 265-279.

Nelson, Joel I. and Robert Grams. 1978b   Worker Union Militance and Occupational Communities. *Rural Sociology.* 17,3: 342-346

Nisbet, Robert A. 1962. *Community and Power: A Study in Ethics of Order and Freedom.* New York and London: Oxford University Press.

_____. 1966. *The Sociological Tradition.* New York: Basic Books.

Oelshlaeger, Max. 1991. *The Idea of Wilderness: From Prehistory to the Age of Ecology.* New Haven: Yale University Press.

O'Laughlin, Jay. 1992. ESA: What the Law Is and What It Might Become. *Journal Of Forestry.* 90,8: 6-12.

Pinchot, Gifford. 1967. *The Fight for Conservation.* Seattle: University of Washington Press.

_____. 1972. *Breaking New Ground.* Seattle: University of Washington Press.

Poggie, John J. and Carl Gersuny. 1974. *Fishermen of Galilee: The Human Ecology of a New England Coastal Community.* Kingston Rhode Island: University of Rhode Island Sea Grant. Marine Bulletin Service Number 17.

Pollnac, Richard B. and John J. Poggie, Jr. 1988. The Structure of Job Satisfaction Among New England Fishermen and its Application to Fisheries Management Policy. *American Anthropologist.* 90,4: 888-901.

Prouty, Andrew Mason. 1973. *Logging with Steam in the Pacific Northwest: The Men, the Camps, and the Accidents.* M.A. Thesis. Department of History, University of Washington, Seattle.

_____. 1982. *More Deadly Than War -- Pacific Coast Logging 1827-1981.* Doctoral Dissertation. Department of History, Seattle: University of Washington.

Raup, Hugh M. 1966. The View from John Sanderson's Farm: A Perspective for the Use of the Land. *Forest History.* (April): 2-11.

Reimer, J. 1977. Becoming a Journey Man Electrician. *Sociology of Work and Occupations.* 4: 87-98.

Richardson, Catherine Woods. 1993. An Analysis of the Socioeconomic Effects of Bureau of Land Management Resource Management Plans in Western Oregon. A Report to the U.S. Department of Interior, Bureau of Land Management, Oregon State Office. Seattle. Institute For Resources in Society, College of Forest Resources, University of Washington.

Robbins, William G. 1988. *Hard Times in Paradise:: Coos Bay, Oregon, 1850-1986.* Seattle: University of Washington Press.

Roberge, Earl. 1991. Timber Country Revisited. Olympia, Washington: Washington Contract Loggers Association.

Robison, W. Henry, Daniel T. Hormaechea and Scott Katzer. 1989. *The Impact of a Reduced Timber Harvest on the Economy of the West-Central Idaho Highlands.* Department of Forest Resources, Moscow, Idaho: University of Idaho.

Salaman, Graeme. 1975. Occupations, Community and Consciousness. *In* Martin Bulmer (ed) *Working Class Images of Society.* London and Boston: Rutledge and Kegan Paul. pp. 219-238.

Salaman, Graeme. 1974. *Community and Occupation: An Exploration in Work/Leisure Relationships.* London: Cambridge University Press.

Sample, V. Alaric and Dennis C. Le Master. 1992a. *Assessing the Employment Impacts of Proposed Measures to Protect the Northern Spotted Owl.* Washington, D.C.: Forest Policy Center, The American Forestry Association.

Sample, V. Alaric and Dennis C. Le Master. 1992b. Economic Effects of Northern Spotted Owl Protection. *Journal of Forestry.* 90(8): 31-35.

Schwantes, Carlos A. 1989. The Pacific Northwest. An Interpretive History. Lincoln Nebraska. University of Nebraska Press.

Schwantes, Carlos A. (In Press) *Hard Traveling: A Portrait of Worklife in the New Northwest.* Lincoln, Nebraska: University of Nebraska Press.

Schwarz and Thompson. 1990. Divided We Stand: Redefining Politics, Technology and Social Choice. Philadelphia, PA: University of Pennsylvania Press.

Scientific Analysis Team. 1993. *Viability Assessments and Management Considerations for Species Associated with Late-Successional and Old-Growth Forests of the Pacific Northwest. USDA Forest Service.* U.S. Government Printing Office (1993-791-566).

Shannon, Margaret A. 1990. Building Trust: The Formation Of A Sccial Contract. In: Lee. Robert G., Donald R. Field and William R Burch, Jr. *Community and Forestry: Continuities in the Sociology of Natural Resources.* Boulder, Colorado. Westview Press.

Society Of American Foresters. 1989. *Report of the Society of American Foresters National Task Force on Community Stability.* Bethesda, Maryland: SAF Resource Policy Series.

Snyder, Gary. 1993. Coming into The Watershed. *In* Scott Walker (ed) *Changing Community.* St Paul, MN: Gray Wolf Press.

Stankey, G. H. 1989. Beyond The Campfire's Light: Historical Roots of the Wilderness Concept. *Natural Resources Journal.* 29(1): 9-24.

Steiner, Fritz, Ingrid Ducchart, Linda Hardesty and William Budd. 1989. *Planning For Agroforestry.* The Hague: Elsiver Science Publishing.

Stevens, Joe B. 1978. *The Oregon Wood Products Labor Force: Job Rationing and Worker Adaptations in a Declining Industry.* Corvallis, Oregon: Oregon State University Agricultural Experiment Station, Special Report. 529pp.

_____. 1979. Six Views About a Wood Products Labor Force, Most of Which May be Wrong. *J. Forestry.* 77 (11): 717-720.

Stier, Jeffrey C. 1982. Changes in the Technology of Harvesting Timber in the United States: Some Implications for Labour. *Agricultural Systems.* 9(4): 255-266.

Strauss, A. and J. Corbin. 1990. *Basics of Qualitative Research: Grounded Theory Procedures and Techniques.* Newbury Park, CA: Sage Publications.

Sykes, A. J. M. 1969a. Navvies: Their Work Attitudes. *Sociology.* 3: 20-35.

_____. 1969b Navvies: Their Social Attitudes. *Sociology.* 3: 157-172.

Taylor, Clive C. and Alan R. Townsend. 1976. The Local Sense of Place as Evidenced in North East England. *Urban Studies.* 13: 133-1465.

Thomas, Jack W. Eric D. Forsman, Joseph B. Lint, E. Charles Meslow, Barry R. Noon, and Jared Verner. 1990. A Conservation Strategy for the Spotted Owl. Portland, Oregon: Interagency Scientific Committee To Address The Conservation Of The Northern Spotted Owl.

Tonnies, F. 1963. *Communities and Society* C. Loomis, (ed). New York: Harper Torchbook Edition.

Tuchmann, E. Thomas. 1994. Personal Communication. Portland, Oregon: U.S. Office of Forestry and Economic Development.

Turnstall, Jeremy. 1962. *The Fishermen.* London: MacGibbon and Kee.

Twight, Ben W. 1983. *Organizational Value and Political Power: The Forest Service vs. the Olympic National Park.* University Park, Pennsylvania and London: University of Oregon Press.

Tyler, Robert L. 1967. *Rebels of the Woods: The I.W.W. in the Pacific Northwest.* Eugene, Oregon: University of Oregon Press.

USDA Forest Service and USDI Bureau of Land Management. 1994. *Final Supplemental Environmental Impact Statement on Management of Habitat for Late-successional and Old-growth Forest Related Species Within the Range of the Northern Spotted Owl.* Portland Oregon: U.S. Government Printing Office.

USDA Forest Service. 1992a. *Final Environmental Impact Statement on Management for the Northern Spotted Owl in the National Forests.* Portland, Oregon: U.S. Government Printing Office.

_____. 1992b. *Caring for the Land and Getting Along with People: Potential Influences of People, Opinion, and Human Nature on Public Land Management.* Washington D.C. USDA Forest Service. Public Affairs Office.

Van Maanen, John and Stephen R. Barley. 1984. Occupational Communities: Culture And Control in Organizations. *Research in Organizational Behavior.* 6: 287-365.

Waggener, Thomas R. 1978. Sustained Yield Policies and Community Stability. Special Paper Presented for Agenda Item 2, The Interaction Between Stability in Forestry and Stability in Communities. 8th World Forestry Congress. Jakarta, Indonesia. October 16-28.

Waggener, Thomas. 1969 Sustained Yield as a Forest Regulation Model. Contribution No. 6, Institute of Forest Products, College of Forest Resources, University of Washington, Seattle.

Walker, David and Steven E. Daniels. 1993. Clinton and the Northwest Forest Conference: A Case of Conflict Mis-management. Paper Presented at The Speech Communication Association Annual Conference. Miami, FL. November.

Warren, Kristin K. 1992. *Role-Making and Coping Strategies among Women in Timber Dependent Communities.* Master's Thesis. College of Forest Resources, Seattle: University of Washington.

Warren, Kristin K., R. G. Lee and M. S. Carroll. 1991. Timber-Dependent Communities in Crisis: Assessing the Roles and Reactions of Women. Paper Presented at the Annual Meeting of the Rural Sociological Society. Columbus, Ohio. August 21.

Warren, Robert L. 1987. *The Community in America.* Chicago: Rand-McNally and Company.

Wellman, D. J. 1987. *Wildland Recreation Policy, An Introduction.* New York: John Wiley and Sons.

Wenzel, George E. 1991. *Animal Rights, Human Rights: Ecology, Economy and Ideology in the Canadian Arctic.* Toranto. University of Toranto Press.

Wilkinson, Charles F. 1992a. *Crossing the Next Meridian. Land, Water, and the Future of the West.* Washington D.C.: The Island Press.

_____. 1992b. *The Eagle Bird: Mapping a New West.* New York: Pantheon.

Wilkinson, Charles F. and H. Michael Anderson. 1987. *Land And Resource Planning in the National Forests.* Washington D.C.: Island Press.

Wilkinson, Kenneth P. 1991. *The Community in Rural America.* New York: The Rural Sociological Society and Greenwood Press. Contributions in Sociology, Number 95.

Williamson, David H. 1976. *Give 'er Snoose: A Study of Kin and Work among Gyppo Loggers of the Pacific Northwest.* Doctoral Dissertation. College of Arts and Sciences, The Catholic University of America, Washington, D.C.

Wirth, Louis. 1938. Urbanism and A Way of Life. *American J. of Sociology.* 44: 1-24.

Wondolleck, J.M. 1988. *Public Lands Conflict and Resolution: Managing National Forest Disputes.* New York: Plenum Press.

Yaffee. 1994. The Wisdon of the Spotted Owl: Policy Lessons for a New Century. Washington, D.C.: Island Press.

Young, John A. and Jan M. Newton. 1980. Taming the Timber Beast. *In* John A. Young and Jan M. Newton. *Capitalism and Human Obsolescence.* New York: Universe Books. pp. 21-56.

INDEX

174

ABOUT THE BOOK
AND AUTHOR

It has often been said that natural resource and environmental problems cannot be solved without solving human problems. In this book, Matthew Carroll examines the economic and social circumstances of northwestern U.S. loggers in the face of shifts in environmental politics, dramatic reductions in timber harvest levels on federal lands, and changing technology and market forces—among other factors that are rapidly transforming their industry, their livelihoods, and their communities.

Drawing upon sociological fieldwork in logging communities that he conducted at various times over a period of nearly a decade and using the spotted owl–old growth controversy as a case study, Carroll provides a rich and detailed picture of life among northwestern loggers. He lays out the human dimensions and dilemmas of the timber crisis. Expanding it from the oversimplified owl-versus-logger confrontation, he puts these issues in a historical and policy context and suggests parallels to other controversies such as public grazing and federal or state river protection. Carroll's work revives the concept of occupational community and shows ways it can be used to understand the dynamics of rural occupations linked to resource extraction.

Matthew S. Carroll is on the faculty in natural resource sciences at Washington State University in Pullman.